RAY CHARLES

"I Was Born With Music Inside Me"

Carin T. Ford

Series Consultant:
Dr. Russell L. Adams, Chairman
Department of
Afro-American Studies,
Howard University

Enslow Publishers, Inc.
40 Industrial Road
Box 398
Berkeley Heights, NJ 07922
USA
http://www.enslow.com

"I WAS BORN WITH MUSIC INSIDE ME.
MUSIC WAS ONE OF MY PARTS. LIKE MY RIBS, MY LIVER,
MY KIDNEYS, MY HEART. LIKE MY BLOOD. . . .
IT WAS A NECESSITY FOR ME—LIKE FOOD OR WATER."
—*Ray Charles*

Library of Congress Cataloging-in-Publication Data

Ford, Carin T.
    Ray Charles : "I was born with music inside me" / Carin T. Ford.
      p. cm. – (African-American biography library)
    Includes bibliographical references and index.
    ISBN-13: 978-0-7660-2701-5
    ISBN-10: 0-7660-2701-5
    1. Charles, Ray, 1930–2004—Juvenile literature. 2. Singers—United States—
Biography—Juvenile literature. 3. African American singers—United States—Biography—
Juvenile literature. I. Title. II. Series.
    ML3930.C443F67 2006
    782.42164092—dc22
    [B]
                                        2006013793

Printed in the United States of America

10 9 8 7 6 5 4 3 2

Illustration Credits: The Associated Press/AP, pp. 38, 49, 61, 86, 106, 109; Courtesy of Rutgers University Institute of Jazz Studies, p. 47; Enslow Publishers, Inc., p. 12; Everett Collection, pp. 77, 91, 103, 105; Florida State Archives, pp. 16, 22, 34; Getty Images, pp. 58, 72; Jupiter Images, pp. 24, 29, 55; The Library of Congress, pp. 4, 18, 46, 70, 74; Time Life Pictures/Getty Images, 64, 94, 98, 100.

Cover Illustrations: The Associated Press/AP (bottom); The Library of Congress (top).

Con

Ray Charles

Chapter 1

Searching for
Success

R ay Charles Robinson stepped off the bus in downtown Seattle, Washington, in March 1948. The seventeen-year-old boy had never been to the city before. In fact, he had never set foot in the western part of the United States. Ray had grown up in Florida and spent his entire life in the South.

Yet now, with both his parents dead, Ray had decided to travel nearly three thousand miles across the country. This would be an adventurous move for any teenager, and it was even more so for Ray. Not only was he an orphan, but he was also blind. However, Ray was determined to make it big as a musician. The extraordinarily talented young pianist and singer had already achieved some fame in the South. In fact, he thought of himself as one of the best musicians in the area.[1] But by moving to Seattle, Ray hoped to become a real success. He wanted his name to become as well known as those of popular singers like Nat King Cole and Charles Brown.

Ray had saved some money over the past couple of years from working with several bands. Gossie McKee, a guitar player and friend of Ray's from Florida, had helped to arrange the Seattle trip. McKee had arrived there

Segregation in America

As African Americans, Ray and McKee were allowed to play only in black nightclubs. Although this was the 1940s, black Americans still were not being treated as equal to whites. They were not allowed to attend the same schools or eat in the same restaurants as whites. In movie theaters, blacks had to sit in a separate section. On buses, such as the one Ray rode from Florida to Washington, black men and women had to sit in the back, while white passengers sat up front. In the South, these rules were followed very strictly. One of the reasons Ray had been interested in traveling north was because he had heard that African Americans were treated better there. While Northerners were generally not as prejudiced as Southerners, African Americans still were often not treated fairly.

before Ray. He had asked a man who worked shining shoes at the bus terminal to direct Ray to the hotel on Jackson Street where McKee was staying. Ray took a cab to the hotel. After resting and eating, he and McKee got down to business.

McKee had been asking around town if there were any job possibilities for the two musicians. The oldest African-American nightclub in Seattle was the Black and Tan. After performing a few songs for the manager, Ray and McKee got a job there, and other jobs quickly followed. Soon, Ray was able to find a place to live and to send for his girlfriend, Louise Mitchell, with whom he had been living in Florida. The couple bought some furniture and found a place to live together.

Making his way around the large city did not seem to be terribly difficult for the blind teenager. He had traveled a lot over the years and was used to memorizing the streets he needed to cross and the stairs he needed to climb to get where he had to go. Ray, who had been blind since the age of seven, had been raised by his mother to be independent. Rather than feeling afraid of being alone, Ray enjoyed his independence. He relied on his other senses, especially hearing, to make his way around. In Florida, he had even spent some of his time riding bicycles and driving cars.

Not long after arriving in Seattle, Ray and Gossie added bass player Milton S. Garret to their ensemble and called themselves the McSon Trio. The name was a combination of Ray's and Gossie's last names, Robinson and McKee. The group played to enthusiastic crowds at the Rocking Chair, a well-known nightclub in the city.

During the fall of 1948, a musician named Jackie McVea heard Ray perform. McVea played tenor saxophone and his song "Open the Door, Richard" recently had been a big hit. He had come to Seattle from Los Angeles, California, to perform at the Washington Social Club. Ray was performing there with the McSon Trio during intermission. One evening, he asked McVea if he could try his sax. Ray had learned how to play the instrument, along with trumpet and clarinet, in school. McVea agreed and was stunned at how well Ray played. The audience went wild over Ray's solo. When McVea arrived back in Los Angeles, he told some people in the recording industry about young Ray Charles Robinson.

A few weeks after McVea's trip to Seattle, the president of Downbeat Records appeared at the Rocking Chair. Jack Lauderdale had heard McVea's praise of Ray and wanted to hear the teenager for himself. Lauderdale listened and told the band that he wanted to record the trio. Although at first the musicians did not believe Lauderdale, they soon realized the man was sincere.

"A record! Man, that was the ultimate," Ray later said. "I had been listening to records my whole life . . . and here I was, actually about to make one."[2]

The McSon Trio showed up at a recording studio in Seattle the following day. They recorded two songs. One song, "I Love You, I Love You," was written by an old friend of Ray's from the Florida School for the Deaf and Blind. The other number, "Confession Blues," had been composed by Ray.

Although Lauderdale was pleased with the songs, he sensed that of the three musicians, he should keep his eye on Ray. Yet he was not happy with Ray's name. At that time, Ray went by the nickname "RC." But Lauderdale did not like the sound of RC Robinson. He suggested dropping the last name and only using the teenager's first and middle names: Ray Charles. Too excited about making a record to give much thought to the name change, Ray agreed.

> "A record! Man, that was the ultimate. I had been listening to records my whole life . . . and here I was, actually about to make one."

In February 1949, the Downbeat record was released. It was a 78—a small disc that turned at a speed of 78 rotations per minute—with one song on each side. Lauderdale had made a few mistakes on the label. He gave Ray credit for writing both numbers, and the trio was listed as the Maxin Trio. However, none of this mattered to the musicians when they saw how well the record sold in Seattle and how the group's popularity grew because of

the recording. "Confession Blues," the song Ray actually wrote, even hit the fifth spot nationally on *Billboard*'s Best Selling Retail Race Records chart in May of that year.

Lauderdale was interested in recording more songs, and the members of the trio were enjoying every minute of their success.

For nineteen-year-old Ray Charles, it was only the beginning.

Chapter 2

Early Hardships

ay Charles Robinson was born on September 23, 1930, in Albany, Georgia. No birth certificate for Ray survives, but he always claimed that September date as his birthday. He was raised in Greenville, Florida, by his mother, Aretha Williams, called Retha, who was only sixteen years old when Ray was born. Ray's father was Bailey Robinson, a tall, muscular man who worked at a log mill and for the railroad. He was not married to Retha and played almost no role in Ray's life. The young girl was left to take care of the baby on her own.

However, she did have the help of a friend in caring for young Ray: Mary Jane Robinson, Bailey Robinson's wife. Together, Mary Jane and Retha acted as mothers to Ray. Mary Jane worked at the sawmill and was the more easygoing of the two women. If Retha wanted to whip Ray

Over the years, Ray lived in different parts of Florida, marked on this map.

when he did something wrong, Mary Jane would step in protectively and prevent her from doing it.

Retha needed a cane to walk and was not physically strong. She was unable to handle work in the sawmill, so she did people's laundry, which she washed and ironed. Retha was very poor.

Retha was a strict mother. She believed that children should do chores and help their families. She also believed in punishing children when they did something wrong.

When Ray was almost two, Retha gave birth to another boy, George. The brothers were very close and enjoyed playing and exploring in the nearby woods. Still, Retha made sure her sons understood the meaning of work. When Ray was five and George four, they had to chop wood and carry water. On Sundays, the family visited the New Shiloh Baptist Church, where African Americans worshiped and sang. Churches—just like schools—were separate for blacks and whites.

As soon as Ray was old enough, he would be able to attend Greenville Training, the public school for African-American children. Ray had a lot of curiosity about the world around him and seemed very bright. He especially enjoyed looking at anything mechanical, from the engines of automobiles to farm machinery.

Yet Ray's earliest memory of what he loved most was music, even though no one in his family played an instrument or could sing. "I was born with music inside me,"

The Great Depression

The early 1930s were difficult times for most Americans. An economic crisis known as the Great Depression began in 1929 and lasted throughout the 1930s. Millions had lost their jobs and many people did not have enough to eat. Being an African American in the South made it even more difficult. At that time, living conditions for blacks were poor, and they did not receive the same level of education as whites. Jobs were hard enough to find in the 1930s and even harder for poorly educated African Americans. Friends and neighbors liked Retha and her cheerful son. They made sure the Robinson family did not starve.

Ray once said. "Music was one of my parts. Like my ribs, my liver, my kidneys, my heart. Like my blood. . . . It was a necessity for me—like food or water. And from the moment I learned that there were piano keys to be mashed, I started mashing 'em, trying to make sounds out of feelings."[1]

That moment came when Ray was little more than three years old. He was playing outside Mr. Pit's Red Wing Café, a general store and restaurant. Suddenly he stopped what he was doing and listened. He heard the sound of piano music. It was Wiley Pitman playing boogie-woogie, a lively style of music based on the blues.

Pitman, who owned the restaurant, could play well and had something of a reputation in the area for his talent. He was particularly accomplished at stride piano, sometimes called "shout" piano. Stride sounded a lot like ragtime, but with a heavier "oom-pah" in the left hand. Thomas "Fats" Waller and James P. Johnson were two of the most famous stride pianists.

The day Ray heard the sounds of boogie-woogie coming from the piano, he ran into the café and soon was sitting on Pitman's lap, his small fingers trying out the piano keys for the first time. Pitman allowed Ray to run his fingers along the keyboard, and the young boy liked the feel of it. "I was a normal kid, mischievous and into everything, but I loved music, it was the only thing that could really get my attention," said Ray.[2]

Ray began visiting the café on a regular basis. Pitman always allowed the child to play the piano and soon taught him the proper way to strike the keys. "He had an old beat-up piano. . . . I'd go over and stand by the piano and listen, and pretty soon he'd move over and make room for me and I'd sit down and bang away up on the high keys," Ray said. "I wasn't playin' nuthin'. He knew it and I knew it, but he'd smile and he'd say, 'Thass good, thass so good, sonny. But you gotta practice.'"[3]

Pitman encouraged Ray's interest in music. In years to come, Ray would call Pitman the man who had the biggest influence on him as a child.

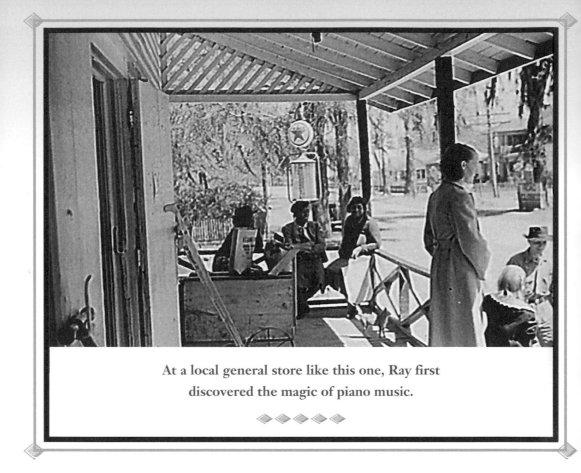

At a local general store like this one, Ray first
discovered the magic of piano music.

Ray enjoyed the time he spent at the café. When he
was not playing piano with Pitman, he was sitting next to
the restaurant's jukebox, listening to the sounds of the
blues, boogie-woogie, and big band music. Sometimes, his
mother's friends would give him a small amount of change
to buy candy. Yet Ray preferred putting the money into
the jukebox and listening to the music he loved. If he was
without money, he would simply wait until someone came

along and put a nickel into the jukebox. "If there was a way to get to listen to music, I'd find it," he said.[4]

In spite of having to get by on so little money, Ray's early years were enjoyable. He loved attending big fish fries and drinking Kool-Aid before heading off to play near the ponds and trees. Retha gave him a birthday party when he turned four, and Ray was excited when he got to eat ice cream, made by hand in an old-fashioned churn. "Didn't bother us any that we were poor," he said. "Didn't bother us 'cause we didn't know any better."[5]

One hot day, an event occurred that would haunt Ray throughout his life. He was playing with his brother, George, near a washtub while Retha was in the house ironing. She used the tub for doing laundry, and it was filled with rinse water. The boys liked to climb into the tub and play in the water. On this day, George climbed in and splashed happily about. All of a sudden, the splashing became frantic. Ray knew that George was in trouble, and yet Ray felt as if he could not move or do anything about it. Overcome by fear, Ray stood rooted to the spot for a few seconds, watching helplessly.

Finally, he ran over to the tub and tugged at his drowning brother. But he was too small to lift George out of the tub. Screaming, Ray ran to the house where his mother was ironing. The distance was not far, yet by the time Retha got to the washtub and pulled George out, the boy was dead. Ray and Retha were horror-stricken.

Ray's mother, like this woman, washed clothes in the yard
in a washtub. But even a few inches of water can spell
danger for young children like Ray and George.

Only a few months after this tragic event, Ray began
to have trouble with his eyes. When he woke up in the
morning, he could barely open them because of mucus
that crusted them shut. Retha bathed Ray's eyes, but he
started losing his eyesight. It was hard for Ray to see
anything far away, and soon even people and objects up
close became blurry.

Retha found a doctor who treated African Americans.
After prescribing some medicine, the doctor told Retha to

take Ray to a clinic in Madison, Georgia. Mother and son traveled nearly fifteen miles to the clinic. There, the doctor informed them that there was no cure for Ray's eye problems. The seven-year-old boy would soon be blind. Today, some doctors think Ray may have been born with an eye disease called glaucoma. If untreated, glaucoma can lead to blindness.

Over the next two years, Ray saw less and less clearly. It did not frighten him because he lost his eyesight slowly. He would awaken with his eyes crusted shut. Once he was able to open them, he would try to adjust to the light. Ray soon lost the ability to see shapes and forms at a distance. Then he began having difficulty seeing anything but large shapes. When even large shapes became blurry, Ray was left with the ability to see colors. Finally, that vanished as well, and all he could make out was night from day. By the age of seven, Ray was totally blind.

Retha had to decide what to do with her son. Young and frail as she was, Retha was a very strong person when it came to making decisions. She knew that if Ray had to go through life blind, she at least could make sure that he had skills and an education. She was determined to make sure Ray was able to stand on his own two feet. She kept telling him that one day she would be gone and Ray would have to take care of himself. She made sure that Ray worked at his chores and learned the alphabet and how to add numbers.

Many of the neighbors did not approve of how Retha was raising Ray. They did not believe he should be using an ax to chop wood or have to help around the house. But Retha knew the day would come when Ray would not have anyone to help him. So she made sure he was able to help himself.

"They almost ran Mama out of town," Ray said about the neighbors. "But she didn't care about them. She cared about me. She would kneel down and say, 'You're blind, not stupid. You lost your sight, not your mind.' And then she'd hug me."[6]

To further Ray's education, Retha needed to find a school for him. Not only would it have to accept African-American children, but it had to cost very little money. She found one in the Florida School for the Deaf and Blind.

Founded in 1885, the school was located in St. Augustine, Florida. The state government would pay Ray's room, board, and tuition as well as his travel expenses. During the trip, the conductor of the train would watch out for the boy. A teacher would be waiting to meet Ray's train after his journey.

It was the perfect arrangement, except for one problem: Ray did not want to go. He did not want to leave his mother, his home, and the people he knew. He cried and cried, but Retha knew that attending the school was in Ray's best interest. At the end of the fall of 1937, Ray said good-bye to his mother and boarded a train for Florida.

Chapter 3

Boarding School

"Man, I was homesick the minute I climbed aboard," Ray said of his journey to the boarding school.[1] He did not feel much better once he arrived. Young Ray was miserable. In spite of the good food and a schedule that kept him busy all day long, he was homesick. His grades were good and he was a fast learner, but the other boys teased him. Everything about life at the Florida School for the Deaf and Blind seemed strange to Ray.

The students followed a strict schedule. They woke up at five-thirty every morning and ate breakfast and attended a church service. Their day was full of classes broken up by lunch and an occasional recess. The children then attended workshops where they learned practical skills such as carving, weaving cane strips into chair seats, making pot holders and leather goods, and putting together

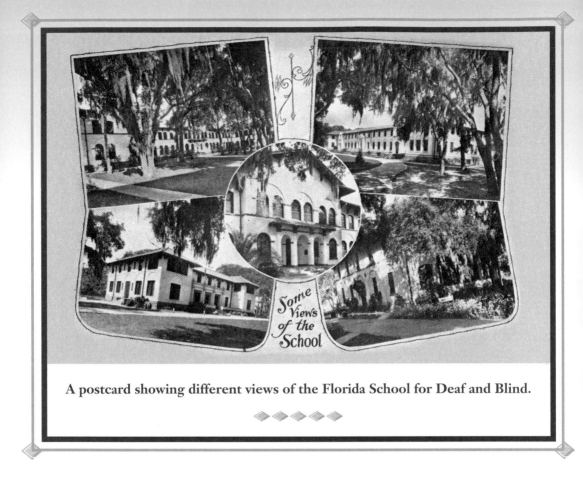

A postcard showing different views of the Florida School for Deaf and Blind.

brooms. The rest of the evening included playtime, dinner, and study hour. It was not hard for Ray to spend his days following such a tight schedule. Retha had raised him to do as he was told, and those lessons served him well at the Florida school.

Ray's teachers began his education by instructing him in Braille, a system of raised dots that allows blind people to read by using their fingertips to feel the different letters. Ray was bright and learned to read Braille in less than two weeks. It did not seem hard to him and soon he was quickly able to read simple stories such as *The White Rabbit* and *Living on John's Farm.*

Boys and girls were housed in separate dormitories; black and white students were kept even farther apart, living on separate campuses. The grounds were divided into North and South Campus. The white children lived on the North Campus. There, equipment such as sewing machines and typewriters was in good repair, the food served was fresh, and the staff received higher pay. Staff members on the South Campus grew the vegetables that were served on the North Campus. The black children on South Campus ate leftovers. The black students used the machines and equipment that were old or broken. Their books written in Braille were worn and in terrible shape. "We got their old Braille books with the bumps so mashed down the children could hardly read them," said one school teacher on South Campus.[2]

Ray may not have realized that the black students were not treated as well as the whites, but he could not help noticing when the boys made fun of him. There were poor children at the Florida School, but Ray was one of the poorest. He had to wear clothes that were donated by the state of Florida, and he was nicknamed "Foots" because he went barefoot.

Ray lived in a state of homesickness his first year. This was made even worse when Ray learned he had to stay at the school over Christmas vacation. The state provided travel expenses only at the beginning and end of the year. Students were responsible for the cost of traveling to and from home during the holidays. Retha did not have enough money to pay for her son's trip home.

Still, the time he was forced to spend alone at the school made Ray realize how much he missed the other students. He had not tried very hard during the first half of the year to be friendly, but he felt very excited when the

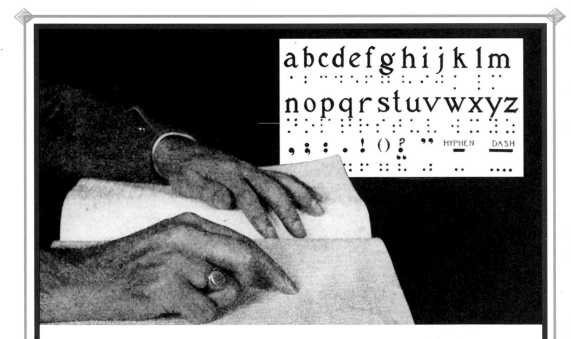

Books and music for blind people are written in Braille. The letters of the alphabet and musical notes in Braille are formed by raised dots. Blind people read Braille by touching the dots with their fingers.

hallways were once again filled with the sounds of noisy boys and girls.

After the holidays, Ray's right eye began giving him problems. The pain was so bad that the doctor at the school decided the eye should be removed. The operation was performed and Ray missed many weeks of classes. When school ended for the year, Ray was finally able to go home.

Back in the town of Greenville, Ray's life picked up where it had left off nine months earlier. He was thrilled to see his mother again. As before, she made sure he was treated like any other boy his age. He continued doing his chores and was punished if he tried to get out of work. Once, he did not want to scrub and mop the floor so he just mopped up some water he had thrown about. When Retha saw what Ray had done, she was furious and made him do the job all over from the beginning.

"Mama was big on those sort of lessons," he said. "She knocked them into my brain with a sledgehammer. She had no choice. I wasn't an easy kid. I was as stubborn and mischievous as any other boy. So she treated me like a naughty puppy and rubbed my nose in my own mistakes."[3]

Most of the time, Ray acted just like any other boy in Greenville. He quickly learned how to ride a bicycle and enjoyed pedaling around at breakneck speed. He was familiar with the roads and pathways that ran through town and possessed a confidence—which stayed with him throughout his life—that made him believe he would not get hurt on the bicycle. He relied on his instincts and his excellent hearing to keep him out of danger.

Ray also resumed spending time with Wiley Pitman at the Red Wing Café. Ray played the piano and listened to the jukebox. Sometimes he was invited into neighbors' homes along with his friend Johnny Williams. The boys would perform gospel music and hymns. As a reward for their playing and singing, the boys were given sandwiches and dessert.

> Ray played the piano and listened to the jukebox.

Back at school in Florida for his second year, Ray felt much more at home. He began making friends and especially enjoyed the games the blind students played. They had their own variation of baseball that involved a rolled up magazine for the ball and a broom handle for a bat. The students would figure out where the "ball" had landed by listening. Then they would run to that area and use their bats to sweep the ground and search for it.

Another activity the blind students participated in was relay races. In order to do this, a wire would be stretched the length of the race's distance. Two boys would run— one on either side of the wire—holding onto the wire as a guide. One of the mean tricks the boys would play on Ray when he was young was to tie one end of the wire to an iron post. Ray would be running as fast as he could and then slam into the post at the end.

Ray enjoyed playing mischief of his own. His most memorable prank was getting behind the wheel of the teacher's car and driving it around the school. Because Ray could not see where to steer the car, a deaf student sat on the hood and gave Ray directions by hitting the car with either his right or left hand. Eventually, the car crashed, tossing Ray into the backseat.

During Ray's second year at the Florida School for the Deaf and Blind, he realized that what he cared about more than anything else was music. On one particular day, Miss Mallard, his music teacher, asked him to play a certain exercise on the piano. Ray was not able to play it well. "You know, there are days when your fingers won't do what they should," he said.[4]

The teacher became angry and hit Ray across his knuckles with a ruler. Furious that anyone would hurt his hands, Ray hit her without even thinking. Mallard went to the principal of the school and told him what had happened. The principal planned to throw Ray out of school for his actions. Yet when Mallard learned of this, she said she thought the punishment was too harsh. She had wanted Ray punished, but not expelled from school.

The experience highlighted to Ray and everyone around him just how important the piano was to him. "I never thought about being famous or rich," he said, "but I did think about being great. I wanted to be a great musician."[5]

The Florida school offered its students three pianos. One was in the girls' practice room, another in the boys' practice room, and a third was in the chapel. Ray spent a lot of time on the boys' practice piano, working on the lessons that were assigned him. Although Ray preferred the sounds of boogie-woogie, he was forced to stick to the classics for the lessons. Ray received a solid grounding in the works of classical composers such as Mozart, Beethoven, and Bach. Yet when his teachers were not around, Ray played blues and jazz while the other students danced to the music.

"I was a classical pianist first. Come on! You think they taught jazz in that school?" he asked. "You played Bach and Beethoven. But that was good. It taught you to play what you think, even though I always wanted to play it some other way than it was written."[6]

Learning to play a musical composition was a long, tedious process, but definitely worth it to Ray. He loved playing the piano, and his intelligence and natural talent enabled him to learn quickly. It was not long before the students and staff at the school recognized Ray as the top pianist. He was often asked to play at school assemblies. These assemblies were held in the school's auditorium. Ray played and sang and accompanied other singers as well. This meant Ray was allowed to perform on the

The Blind Piano Student

For Ray, as for the other blind students at the school, learning a piece of music was all about memorization. A piano student who can see reads the sheet music  while keeping his fingers on the keys. A blind student cannot read music unless it is in Braille, and Braille music requires a students to place at least one hand on the music to feel the bumps that represent the different notes.

Ray would learn a couple of bars at a time, one hand at a time, and memorize the notes he needed to play before moving on. For example, he would keep his left hand on the Braille music, reading the notes that his right hand needed to play. He would keep his right hand on the keyboard and play the notes until he had memorized them. He would then switch and put his left hand on the keys and his right hand on the music. Finally, when he had memorized the notes, he would play the bars with both hands together. Sometimes he memorized as many as two thousand bars of music at one sitting.

"good" piano. Sometimes, with another student on the drums, Ray would perform at school social events, which celebrated various holidays.

Practice time, however, was still restricted to the one boys' piano and it was not always easy to get a chance to play on it. Many of the students wanted to use the piano. One time, Ray became very annoyed when another student continually nagged him to get off the piano. When Ray was finished playing, he removed all the keys and took them away to his room, leaving only the piano—without a keyboard—in the room.

Ray was now able to go home over the holidays. Each staff member donated some money so Ray could buy a train ticket to Greenville. At home, Retha continued to make sure her son did not feel sorry for himself. As always, she tried to impress upon him the importance of an education so that he could live his life as an independent man. She told him that along with going to school, he needed some "plain horse sense" to get by in the world.[7]

Although Ray enjoyed his visits home during the winter and summer holidays, he grew restless as the years passed. A married couple that used to live in Greenville invited the young teenager to visit Tallahassee, Florida, during one of these vacations. Ray had a great time in Tallahassee. He had ridden a bicycle many times at home, using the sound and feel of dirt under his tires to guide him. In Tallahassee, he rode a motorbike behind a friend.

He listened to the sound of the motorbike in front of him and simply followed behind.

Ray had determined from a very young age that his blindness would never force him to depend on anyone else. "There were three things I never wanted to own," he said, "a dog, a cane, and a guitar. In my brain, they each meant blindness and helplessness . . . I didn't want to have to depend upon anyone or anything other than myself."[8]

> "There were three things I never wanted to own, a dog, a cane, and a guitar."

To Ray, learning his way around a new city was like memorizing a piece of music. All that was needed was to take it one step—or one bar—at a time. He was always confident. When he walked, he walked quickly.

But most important, that summer Ray began playing with a band in Tallahassee run by Lawyer Halliburton Smith. The band, which consisted of up to eight musicians, played most weekends at cafés, parties, proms, and weddings. They were so popular and well thought of that they played at the Governor's Ball each New Year's Eve. Ray played the piano and sometimes sang. Whereas at school he occasionally had gotten into trouble for singing songs with sexy lyrics, he was able to perform these numbers with Smith's band. The audience, especially the women, loved it.

> "Nothing had hit me like that. Not George drowning. Not going blind. Nothing."

Ray felt restless when he returned to school. His experiences in Tallahassee had been fun and exciting. He had been able to do the thing he loved most—play the piano and sing—and he had been able to concentrate on it. School was not nearly as interesting, although as Ray's reputation grew, he played a number of jobs in the city of St. Augustine. Once, he performed live on a local radio station and got into an argument with the conductor of the radio's orchestra. Ray told him that a violinist was slightly off pitch and sounded flat. The conductor, who was white, became angry at having an African-American teenager criticize one of his musicians. Yet when he finally listened to the violinist, he discovered Ray was right.

At school, Ray sang in the choir as well as with another small group organized by the students themselves. The youngest in the group, Ray had grown up with gospel music. In later years, it would figure heavily in his music.

School dragged on for Ray until, for the second time in his young life, he had to deal with a tragedy in his family. His mother, Retha, died at the age of thirty-one, leaving fifteen-year-old Ray alone in the world. It is not known why she died. The grief Ray felt nearly overwhelmed him. "Nothing had hit me like that," he said. "Not George drowning. Not going blind. Nothing."[9]

BOARDING SCHOOL

he couldn't see anyway!

Ray traveled home to Greenville. He did not eat, talk, or cry. He was numb and barely able to function. He could not imagine that he would never see his mother again. "When she went, I couldn't eat, couldn't swallow," he said. "Couldn't cry. I was completely out of it."[10]

With the help of family friends, Ray was able to overcome the numbness. He said good-bye to his mother at her funeral and spent the summer trying to figure out what he would do next. Music still played an important role in his life, and he again visited Tallahassee to play with Lawyer Smith's band. Yet he kept wondering where he should go and what he should do.

With the death of his mother, Ray had lost the feeling that Greenville was home. When he returned to the Florida School for the Deaf and Blind in the fall, he felt out of place. He did not believe that staying in school would help him in any way. He purposely talked back to teachers and behaved badly. When school officials told Ray in October 1945 that he was being expelled, Ray replied that they did not need to expel him—he was quitting.

By the time he had packed his bags and left the school, Ray had made two decisions: he would move to Jacksonville, Florida, and he would somehow make a living as a musician.

Ray was only fifteen when he went to Jacksonville, Florida, above.
"I just wanted to play music," he said.

◆◆◆◆◆

Chapter 4

On His
Own

ay had decided to head to Jacksonville,
Florida. Just before leaving Greenville, a
group of town residents—all white—
approached Ray. They wanted to buy him a
Seeing Eye dog, an animal trained to help the blind. Ray
did not have to think twice. He told them no. Although
his confidence often came close to stubbornness, Ray was
determined to handle everything on his own. Retha had
taught him to stand on his own two feet, and Ray meant
to do just that. "I'd rather stumble a little and maybe bang
my knee once or twice—just the way sighted people do—
than be dependent on a four-legged canine," he said.[1]

An old friend of Ray's mother told him he would be
able to live in Jacksonville with some friends of hers, Fred
and Lena Mae Thompson. The Thompsons lived in an
African-American section of the city called La Villa. The

couple did not have any children, and they welcomed Ray. They were eager to do all they could for the blind teenager. They wanted to feed him well, buy him new clothes, and give him an allowance.

Much as Ray enjoyed the warmth of the Thompson's home, he was not interested in handouts. He intended to earn his living as a musician. Fred Thompson took Ray to the musician's union, a short distance from their house.

Ray spent much of his time at Local 632 during his first weeks in Jacksonville. He paid attention to the older musicians, determined to learn exactly what it took to become a successful professional musician. Ray had received solid musical training at the Florida School for the Deaf and Blind, but it had been rooted in the classics. The kind of music he needed to know to play with bands in nightclubs was jazz, as well as the blues and popular music. He needed to know the dozens of songs that audiences requested night after night. He had to learn chord progressions, and he had to be able to change key without even thinking about it.

The Musicians' Union

Local 632 was the union for African Americans who belonged to the American Federation of Musicians. A musician needed to be a member of the union in order to get hired to play in any of the bands in the area. Many musicians were used as occasional substitutes in a particular band. But sometimes these temporary spots would become permanent.

Ray hung around the musicians' union, listening and learning. Yet whenever he was allowed to take a seat at a piano, he worked with other musicians to learn whatever he needed to know.

Ray was only fifteen, and some of the older musicians resented him. Sometimes, the veteran musicians purposely tried to throw him off, hoping to confuse him and force him into making mistakes. If Ray wanted to cut it as a professional musician, he had to prove himself. He had to show he could do anything that was asked of him.

There were times when Ray felt discouraged, but he never gave up. "When I left school, I didn't know what a career was," Ray said. "I just wanted to play music, anywhere, and maybe make a few bucks. I never set my stakes past getting food for the next week."[2]

Working hard, he was gradually able to hold his own with the more-seasoned performers, and soon he began getting jobs. Ray slowly developed a reputation as the pianist who was able to play and sing in the style of the popular performers of the day, Nat King Cole and Charles Brown.

Like Ray, Nat King Cole had been exposed to music at an early age and played the piano as a young boy. Cole had formed his first jazz band in high school, but his career really took off with the King Cole Trio. A singer with a voice like velvet, Cole became most famous for such

At first, Ray built his reputation
on being able to sing like
the popular Nat "King" Cole.

songs as "Mona Lisa," "Unforgettable," and "Rambling Rose."

Charles Brown had been raised by his grandmother, who encouraged him to study classical piano when he was ten years old. Brown, however, enjoyed blues and jazz. He became a vocalist and pianist for the Three Blazers when he was in his twenties. The group's sound was heavily influenced by the blues, while still modeling itself after Nat King Cole's trio. Brown eventually went solo. His mellow singing style and extraordinary talent as a pianist made Brown a popular performer who frequently had songs on the top of the rhythm and blues charts.

Ray was heavily influenced by both Cole and Brown, both of whom were well-known musicians when Ray was trying to break into the business.

He was asked to play fairly often at the Two Spot club with drummer Henry Washington's band. Washington was a top musician in Jacksonville, and he was aware of Ray's talent.

Tiny York was a well-known tenor sax player who also sang in the area and had his own ensemble. When he put together a tour for his band throughout Florida, he asked Ray to come along as the pianist and featured vocalist. Ray accepted the offer and was soon sitting on a bus with the band, heading 150 miles toward Orlando.

Once in Orlando, Tiny York's band played a few jobs until the musicians found themselves out of work. They were not getting hired and Tiny decided to travel back to Jacksonville. Ray, however, chose to stay in Orlando. He thought perhaps there might be some opportunities for his talents.

Work did not come quickly or easily and Ray found himself poorer than he had ever been in his life. "There was a lot of days when I had nothin' to eat, but you do learn how to take care of yourself, even when you're too proud and you don't wanna ask nobody for nothin'," he said later.[3]

He could not afford food and sometimes became dizzy from going days at a time without anything to eat. On a good day, he ate a few sardines and a handful of crackers. At this time, Ray learned that his father, Bailey Robinson, had died. Even though Ray had not had a relationship with his father, he felt more alone than ever.

Ray was living in a boardinghouse and promised to pay the landlady the three-dollars-a-week rent as soon as he had a job. Meanwhile, the sixteen-year-old Ray made his way around the city, meeting musicians and visiting nightclubs.

"When I wasn't working, when I went hungry, I kept feeling, somehow if I just played, even for nothing, well, I'd get something," he said. "I would play for free and say [to the club owners], 'If you make anything and you want to give me something, OK.' I needed to eat. My motivation was the music. You can forget a lot of things if you wrap yourself in music."[4]

After a while, Ray was asked to play in the Sunshine Club band. This was the resident band of a club owned by Joe Anderson. Happy to have a job playing the piano, Ray asked Anderson if he might try his hand at writing arrangements for the group. He had done this at the Florida School for the Deaf and Blind, and now Anderson gave him the chance to try it at the professional level.

It was an outstanding opportunity for Ray. Now, he could offer his services as an arranger, and as a vocalist and pianist, too. The fact that arranging music was harder for Ray because he was blind did not bother him in the least. He dictated the specific notations to another musician.

"I see and hear the chords in my mind. I don't use Braille music," he said. "I just call out the notes—instrument by instrument—for everyone in the band. I keep a sound picture in my head."[5]

If the music did not sound exactly the way Ray wanted, he would make the necessary changes at rehearsal.

Anderson liked what Ray was doing, and Ray continued working on arrangements for the band to perform. Since he was working regularly, he now had a little money to spend. He treated himself to a record player and spent hours listening to the big names in jazz such as vocalist Billie Holiday, trumpeter Dizzy Gillespie, and alto saxophone player Charlie Parker. Ray began playing alto saxophone himself and composed a song called "Confession Blues."

> Ray began playing alto saxophone himself and composed a song called "Confession Blues."

Ray seemed at home in Orlando. He had steady work, enjoyed playing the piano in the Southland Music Store where he also bought records, and was often seen riding his bicycle or walking along the busy sidewalks, always able to navigate his way without stumbling or running into anyone.

One day, when Ray was almost seventeen, Lucky Millinder and his band arrived in Orlando to play at the Sunshine Club. Millinder's band toured throughout the country and was well known, ranking only slightly below stars such as Duke Ellington.

When Ray heard that Millinder was looking to hire a pianist, he decided, with the encouragement of friends, to audition for the spot. Ray played and Millinder listened. When Ray was finished, the bandleader told him, "Ain't good enough, kid."[6]

Ray was devastated. For weeks he cried, nursing the secret worry that Millinder could be right. But worry did not mean defeat; Ray was not ready to give up. After spending three-quarters of a year in Orlando, he decided to leave with some friends and head for Tampa.

The decision turned out to be a good one. He quickly landed jobs with two bands: Charlie Brantley's Honeydrippers and the Florida Playboys. Only Ray's

> "Ain't good enough, kid."

talent on the piano was needed with the Honeydrippers; the band already had a vocalist. He played and sang with the Playboys. In fact, he even learned to yodel for one number. The Playboys were a country band made up of white musicians. The group naturally played in clubs with white audiences. In 1947, having a black musician in the band might have been a problem. Yet Ray experienced little trouble and stayed with the Playboys for several months.

He was now earning more money than he had ever made in his life—up to twenty dollars a night with the Playboys and ten dollars with the Honeydrippers. Ray sent most of his money home to a bank in Greenville.

Around this time, Ray fell in love with Louise Mitchell, who was sixteen. Her parents did not approve of the relationship. In protest, Ray and Louisa ran off briefly to Miami and returned to Tampa only when Louise's parents agreed that they could live together.

A new club opened up in Tampa called the Skyhaven Club. Ray was asked to join the Manzy Harris Quartet which played a regular spot at the Skyhaven. Ray could do an accurate impersonation of Nat King Cole, whose popularity throughout the country was enormous. Ray's act was a huge success. The Manzy Harris Quartet played to a full house every weekend and much of the band's popularity was due to Ray's presence.

During the winter of 1948, Gossie D. McKee, the guitar player of the band, started talking to Ray about the two of them leaving Florida and getting out of the South. McKee felt sure that with Ray's talent on piano and vocals, the two men could become successful in the North where living conditions were better for African Americans.

At first, Ray was not interested. Not only was he something of a star in Tampa, but he was making steady money. And then there was Louise. The couple was in love. Ray did not want to simply pack up and leave her.

McKee continued trying to persuade Ray to leave Tampa. Finally, Ray, who was always interested in a challenge, agreed. The musicians decided to head for Seattle, Washington. McKee left a week earlier, giving Ray time to say good-bye to Louise. McKee also had Ray's collection of records with him. These acted as insurance in case Ray got cold feet about making the trip. McKee knew Ray would never abandon his records. Ray told Louise he would send for her as soon as he could.

"Moving on was my main item, and nothing could stop me once my mind was made up," he said. "I've always been pigheaded that way. Got to go and do what I want to do, what I think is right for me."[7]

Ray felt he had accomplished all he was going to in Florida. He did not think he was ready for bigger and more sophisticated cities like New York and Chicago. He thought Seattle would be a place he could manage more easily and not feel so lost.

Ray boarded the bus with five hundred dollars in one of his bags. He had not told anyone about the money. It was there for safekeeping.

In March 1948, seventeen-and-a-half-year-old Ray Charles arrived in Seattle.

Chapter 5

On the Move

 ossie McKee had spent his time alone in Seattle talking to people around the city and drumming up jobs for himself and Ray. There was not much need for a lone guitarist. But a guitar player with a pianist who could also sing was a different story.

Ray and McKee soon found themselves playing to enthusiastic audiences in some of Seattle's most popular black nightclubs. They added bass player Milton Garret and called themselves the McSon Trio. Rather than sit back, satisfied with what he was accomplishing, Ray continued learning and developing his sound. Musicians came at all hours to the house he shared with Louise, who had joined him. By this time, Ray had bought his first piano. It was a small electric piano that cost about two hundred dollars, and he loved it. Often, Ray would leave his house,

Ray arrived in Seattle in 1948.

which was filled with musicians, to perform with McKee at a nightclub. When he would return hours later, Ray would take his seat once again at the piano and join in the music.

While there were many wonderful and exciting things happening in Ray's life at this time, there was a downside as well. Drugs were commonly used by the musicians in the nightclub scene. The bass player of the McSon Trio, Milt Garret, was a heavy drinker and a heroin addict. Although McKee was not interested in trying drugs, Ray was. He was surrounded by musicians using marijuana, cocaine, and heroin and he wanted to experience them. At first, no one was interested in introducing Ray to drugs. He was only a boy. Plus, he was blind. It did not seem right. But eventually Ray got his way, and he moved quickly from marijuana to heroin. For many years to come, drugs would play a major role in Ray's life. Yet he always took full responsibility for the harm he was causing his body.

Quincy Jones

One musician who came frequently to Ray's house was Quincy Jones. Jones was fifteen years old and had recently moved to Seattle with his family. The high school student played the trumpet. He greatly admired Ray, who was already a successful professional,

Quincy Jones

although the two were close in age. Jones was interested in arranging and came to Ray for advice. Ray gladly helped him, and a close friendship grew between the two teenagers. Jones went on to become a musical arranger, record producer, and film composer, and would win more than twenty-five Grammy Awards.

"I did it to myself," he said. "It wasn't society that did it to me, it wasn't a pusher, it wasn't being blind or being black or being poor. It was all my own doing."[1]

The McSon Trio recorded two songs for Downbeat Records and watched with delight as the record sold well in the Seattle area. Ray's song, "Confession Blues," made the best-selling charts nationwide in the spring of 1949 and stayed there until July. Jack Lauderdale, president of Downbeat, asked for more.

In June 1949, the group recorded seven more songs, both blues and ballads. They waited throughout the summer for some word of their new record. None came, but Lauderdale sent some money and two tickets for a flight to Los Angeles, Downbeat's home base. Ray and McKee decided since they were the two original musicians of the group, they should be the ones to travel to Los Angeles. For two days and nights, Ray and McKee spent their time in the recording studio. The two men then made their way back to Seattle and the trio resumed playing at clubs in the area.

But Ray was now thinking beyond Seattle. He had discovered that he could arrive in a strange city, make contacts and find work. Lauderdale had been talking to him about coming to L.A. on his own and Ray was interested. Ray had always dreamed of making it big and now it seemed as if this was his chance. However, it was a big move and he questioned whether he should make it.

Some of the tension Ray was feeling spilled over into his relationship with Louise. They began fighting until finally Louise took a bus home to be with her parents in Tampa, Florida.

Ray moved into a hotel room and started using drugs even more heavily than before. When Lauderdale told Ray he wanted to record him with a big band, Ray decided to take the offer. Without telling McKee, Ray took off

Ray Charles hit Jackson Street in 1948 at the age of 17. He soon led a trio with a steady club gig, a radio show and a TV show. In 1950 Charles left on tour with blues star Lowell Fulson. **57**

Ray Charles with Maxin Trio, circa 1948–4.
Courtesy of Museum Young

Years later, the city of Seattle would be proud to claim Ray as one of its own. Shown here is a museum display with some memorabilia from his time there.

❖ ❖ ❖ ❖ ❖

for Los Angeles. Months away from his twentieth birthday, he was ready for the big time.

Lauderdale put Ray to work right away. Ray recorded several songs for the Swingtime label (formerly known as Downbeat, the name was changed to avoid confusion with *Down Beat* magazine). "Late in the Evening" and "Th' Ego Song" were selected as the first to be released. Ray was known in local newspapers as the "blind piano sensation" and just as he had in Florida and Washington, Ray soon felt at home in Los Angeles. He met Loretta, a woman who worked at Swingtime, and the two began living together. But he also spent time with other women, a pattern he would follow throughout his life.

Ray met top performers such as Art Tatum, who was considered the best jazz pianist around. Confident as he was, Ray stood speechless as he heard Tatum play. He had admired Tatum for years, ever since he had first listened to his records. Although Ray's interests led him to singing, composing, and arranging music, he still considered Tatum the model of all a jazz pianist could be.

Ray was enjoying himself, yet he continued the habit of heavy drug use. He went on a tour that summer through the Southwest with Lowell Fulson, the guitar player and singer with whom he had recorded "Late in the Evening." Fulson was nine years older than Ray. Together they traveled to Oklahoma, Arizona, Louisiana, and Texas. Occasionally, other musicians joined the group.

Ray was attracting a lot of attention. Wherever he went, it seemed his name got mentioned in the local newspaper. Not only was his piano playing brilliant, but his singing ability brought something special to each performance.

"I sing with all the feeling I can put into it, so that I can feel it myself," he said.[2] It was not long before Ray became the band's musical director. He wrote out the arrangements for the band's songs and was so happy with what he was doing, he did not charge Fulson for his extra work. "I was too busy being happy," he said. "Here I was—traveling, playing before people, recording, singing as a solo act, all at a very young age."[3]

Lauderdale tried recording Ray with a big band behind him. But sales of the record were not as high as his original release, "Confession Blues." So Lauderdale decided to go back to fewer musicians playing with Ray for a quieter, more personal sound. Ray still was playing music following the styles of Nat King Cole and Charles Brown. Yet one of the songs he recorded, "Baby Let Me Hold Your Hand," had a lot more of Ray Charles Robinson in it, and Lauderdale was fairly sure he had something special with this song.

He planned to release the number in January 1951 and asked Ray to go on tour again to create interest in the upcoming record. So Ray and Fulson went back on the

> "I sing with all the feeling I can put into it, so that I can feel it myself."

road, playing to crowds that were even larger and more enthusiastic than on their previous tour.

The tour took Ray and the other musicians from the northern cities of Philadelphia and Cleveland down south to New Orleans and Atlanta, and then west to Los Angeles.

Ray's recording of "Baby Let Me Hold Your Hand" had been released and was slowly working its way up *Billboard*'s rhythm and blues jukebox chart, where it eventually reached the number-eight spot. "Baby Let Me Hold Your Hand" sold considerably more records than "Confession Blues" had a couple of years earlier.

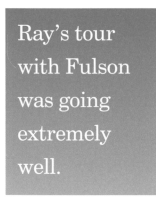

Ray's tour with Fulson was going extremely well.

Ray's tour with Fulson was going extremely well. In April 1951, Ray signed a management contract with Shaw Artists. The young up-and-coming company would keep Ray supplied with jobs for well over a decade.

All the touring meant a lot of time on a bus. Ray, Fulson, and the other musicians passed the time by talking, sleeping, playing cards, and gambling on dice games. Ray could tell the numbers on the dice by feeling the bumps with his fingers.

Ray also spent a lot of his time thinking. For years now he had been imitating some of the nation's most popular African-American performers.

"One morning," Ray said, "I woke up and, still laying in bed, something said to me, 'Where is Ray Charles? Who knows your name? Nobody ever calls you, they just say, Hey kid, you sound like Nat Cole,' but they don't even know your name."[4]

He wondered if perhaps the time had come to stop imitating others and start focusing on his own sound.

Chapter 6

A Sound of His Own

Touring gave Ray Charles a chance to do something he had always enjoyed: meeting women. In Cleveland, during the summer before Charles turned twenty-one, he met Eileen Williams, a hairstylist. Only weeks later, the couple decided to get married.

The tour made its way south to New Orleans before heading back to Los Angeles by October. Charles was earning good money now and continuing his habit of putting a portion of it away in his savings account in Greenville. He also decided, when the tour had ended, that he would be more comfortable traveling around the country in a car rather than a bus. He bought an Oldsmobile and paid a driver to sit behind the wheel.

Charles's musicianship had helped shape the tour band into a smoothly functioning rhythm and blues ensemble.

Because the music sprang from African-American roots and was performed by black musicians, there were traditionally few white listeners. Segregation was a part of American life throughout the first half of the twentieth century, and music was segregated as well. In the early 1950s, white teenagers began listening to radio stations that played music performed by black artists. "You could segregate schoolrooms and buses, but not the airwaves," said one broadcasting executive.[1]

In this way, music lovers across the United States—both black and white—were introduced to rhythm and blues.

Rhythm and Blues

In 1949, *Billboard* magazine began using the term "rhythm and blues." It described the music made by African-American musicians for black audiences. Rhythm and blues bands usually featured a lead singer and a lead instrumentalist supported by a  rhythm section, which contained a double bass or bass guitar, drums, and a keyboard. The lyrics often had to do with love. Yet the main focus of the music was the rhythm; this was music a person could dance to.

At Swingtime Records that fall, Lauderdale recorded the band playing four songs Charles had written: "Kissa Me Baby," which eventually hit number eight on the rhythm and blues charts, "Hey Now"; "The Snow Is Falling"; and "Misery in My Heart."

Another tour began as 1951 drew to a close. The driver of Charles's Oldsmobile had to race to catch up with the tour bus because Charles had been busy buying enough heroin to last him the trip. In the car, Charles made sure he had a record player to listen to the blues, jazz, gospel, and country songs he enjoyed. He also helped pass the travel time by listening to the radio. Eileen did not like life on the road and went back to work as a hair-stylist in her hometown of Columbus, Ohio.

Meanwhile, Swingtime Records had come upon hard times financially. Lauderdale was forced to sell Charles's recording contract to Atlantic Records. Recording with a bigger company would help Charles's career.

Early 1952 saw Charles and the rest of the band touring in the Northeast. They played in some of the top clubs and theaters where African-American musicians performed. They played in Philadelphia, Harlem, New York, Cleveland, and Chicago.

By the end of the tour, Charles and the other musicians were aware that Lowell Fulson was the bandleader in name only. Charles arranged and wrote the music, rehearsed the group, and was the main reason why the band drew large crowds to its performances. When Fulson refused to give Charles an increase in salary, Charles felt that he was being taken advantage of and he quit the band.

Charles was now on his own, in more ways than one. His marriage had fallen apart. While Charles had been on tour, Eileen had begun drinking. Even though Charles himself used alcohol and drugs, he did not want his wife to drink. The marriage was over.

Charles was able to continue touring with other musicians and he also began recording with Atlantic Records. The executives for Charles's new recording label had high hopes for their new musician. Yet Charles's first record had disappointing sales. The two songs on it were "Midnight Hour" and "Roll with My Baby" and followed Charles's style of imitating Charles Brown and Nat King Cole.

The executives at Atlantic knew—just as Charles knew—that he needed to find his own sound. "My Mom taught me one thing, 'Be yourself, boy.' And that's the premise I went on," he said.[2]

Yet the search to discover who he was, and what his sound was, continued. In the meantime, Charles went back on the road. For the next couple of years, his life was a combination of performing throughout the country and recording. His songs, such as

> "My Mom taught me one thing, 'Be yourself, boy.'"

At last Ray was developing his own distinctive sound.

"Mess Around" and "Funny But I Still Love You," were receiving good reviews from critics, but still he had not turned out a hit. Charles was as anxious for this to happen as the Atlantic executives. They knew Charles was an outstanding musician. His music was developing; he was working toward finding his own style. They patiently waited.

One aspect of Charles's life that interested most people who knew him was how easily he made his way around cities he could not see. Charles explained that he always wore shoes with hard heels. Like a bat, he would listen to the echo his heels made. He could tell from the echo if he was approaching a wall or an open space.

While twenty-three-year-old Charles was in Houston, he met a woman named Della Beatrice Howard. She was a singer with the Cecil Shaw Singers, one of Charles's favorite gospel groups. A year older than Charles, Howard was a quiet, family-oriented woman. For all Charles's interest in other women, part of him craved the love and security he had felt as a boy when he lived with Retha and Mary Jane. He had left that behind at a young age, and Howard seemed to bring that warm feeling with her. She and Charles were attracted to each other from their first meeting and when Charles went back on tour, he wrote Howard love letters on his Braille typewriter.

Charles's travels now took him once again to Los Angeles and then to the northeast part of the country. The records he had recorded the previous year ("The Things I Used to Do" and "It Shoulda Been Me") were starting to sell well. "The Things I Used to Do" even climbed to the top spot on the rhythm and blues charts. He still was not the red-hot success Atlantic hoped for, but he was getting there.

Around this time, Mary Jane Robinson died. Charles had looked on her as his second mother and he grieved at her passing.

Meanwhile, Charles was becoming more and more interested in putting together his own band. He wanted a regular group of musicians he could rely on and rehearse with to get the kind of tight sound he was looking for. He asked his manager at Shaw Artists to let him put a group together. But Billy Shaw was reluctant. For one thing, Charles was young; running a band was not easy. For another, Charles's drug use made him a bad risk. Who knew when he might get arrested for using heroin and marijuana?

Charles kept pestering Shaw for his own band. One night in Philadelphia, he became especially annoyed when the musicians he was playing with were not able to follow him. "That band was so bad I went back to my hotel and cried," Charles said.[3]

He finally got his chance to form his own band that summer of 1954. Singer Ruth Brown was scheduled to perform at various clubs throughout Texas and she needed a band behind her. Since it would be for only a two-week period, Shaw agreed to give Charles the opportunity.

Charles quickly decided to form a seven-man band. He wanted bass, percussion, piano, two saxophones, and two trumpets. As Charles looked to hire musicians, he made sure they could read music and did not just play by ear.

Ray's band later traveled around the country in his personal tour bus.

Once he had gathered his musicians, Charles rehearsed the band during the day in a Houston club. The musicians soon discovered that Charles would work them hard—as hard as he worked himself. "Off the bandstand he's nice, but on the stand he's a horse of a different color," said Jimmy Bell, a bass player.[4]

The group performed well behind Ruth Brown and soon was making its way to Cleveland and then Los Angeles. Trumpet player Renald Richard was paid an extra five dollars a week to take down dictation, as Charles called out every note he wanted each instrument to play.

While traveling with the band in late 1954, Charles and Richard were listening to the radio one evening and heard a lively gospel song. At first they sang along with it, but soon they began improvising and calling out their own lyrics. The result was the gospel-blues song "I Got a Woman." The combination of the two styles of music was something new. Charles was so pleased with the results that he asked the Atlantic executives to come down to Atlanta and record the number, along with a few other songs.

In "I Got a Woman," Charles gave gospel music a rhythm and blues sound, something that had not been done before. The executives were sure "I Got a Woman" would be the hit for which they had waited so long.

Chapter 7

Higher and Higher

The record executives were right. "Ray just seemed to be another rhythm-and-blues singer," said Jerry Wexler of Atlantic Records about Charles's style before "I Got a Woman." "But he suddenly broke out of a cocoon that we didn't even know he was weaving."[1]

The song became a true national hit. "When I wrote this song . . . I decided now is the time," he said. "Either you're going to sink or swim. So at that point I just said, 'Hey, this is what I'm going to do and if I'm going to be accepted, good, and at least if I'm not going to be accepted, I'll know that, too."[2]

Charles let the real power of his voice come through on the recording and "I Got a Woman" is often considered the first soul song. Charles had found his sound.

Charles toured with his band through the South and Midwest. He had full command of the stage when he

Ray liked to lean away from the piano and sway to the
music as he played. He always wore sunglasses.

performed. He always wore sunglasses and he liked to lean away from the piano and sway as he played. His voice was distinctive, producing a gravelly yet amazingly flexible sound that occasionally traveled into falsetto, which is when a man's voice hits the upper register beyond its normal range. According to Ahmet Ertegun, cofounder of Atlantic Records, Charles had "that thrilling, amazing and soulful voice."[3]

When he returned to Texas for more performances, Charles spent time with Della, who was pregnant and due to have the baby in a few months. The couple got married on April 5, 1955, in Dallas. They rented a house on a quiet street. Charles made sure Della would have everything she needed, such as credit at the local grocery store, since he would be traveling much of the time.

Della loved Charles and she continued loving him in spite of his heroin addiction and his continued interest in other women. In Charles's mind, he lived two lives: on the road and off the road. He kept the two worlds apart and told Della they needed to respect each other's privacy.

With "I Got a Woman" still selling well in the spring, Charles recorded four more songs at a radio station in Miami, Florida, where he had been performing. There were two slow blues songs, "Hard Times" and "A Fool for You," while "A Bit of Soul" was a lively number that moved from blues to rock and roll. "This Little Girl of

Mine" was based on a gospel song and with Charles's arrangement, had a Latin flavor.

While on tour in Kentucky, Charles met blues singer Mary Ann Fisher. She asked if she could perform a song with the band. Charles was reluctant to agree until he heard her voice. Then he asked her to join them. Not only did Charles like having a singer with the band, he liked Mary Ann in particular. Married for only one month, Charles entered into a relationship with Mary Ann. In May, he left the tour briefly for a few days when Della had the baby. Ray Charles Robinson Jr. was born on May 25, 1955.

Charles was juggling a lot but maintained his jam-packed schedule. He was always sure of himself and how he wanted things done. At one recording session, Jerry Wexler made several suggestions. Charles eventually banged his hands on the piano and said, "If I'm gonna do a session, I'm gonna do it my . . . way, or I ain't gonna do it at all."[4]

"I Got a Woman" stayed on the charts until the start of June. It was at this time that "A Fool for You" and "This Little Girl of Mine" were released, both climbing up the charts and staying there for four months. Charles's third hit record debuted in October. The songs on the two sides were "Greenback" and "Black Jack." If Charles was not yet a big-time celebrity, his reputation was certainly growing with three hit records in a row.

A Tough Bandleader

Charles consistently took full control of the musicians who worked for him. He demanded the best from the members of his band, just as he demanded it of himself. If a musician did not perform well—usually because of drinking—Charles would give him one more chance and warn, "If that ever happens again, you're out. No questions, no discussions, no pleading, no second chances. . . . That's just how Mama had it with me."[5]

No matter how well known he was becoming, Charles was not above the law. On tour in Philadelphia one night, Charles and three other musicians locked themselves in a dressing room to get high on drugs before the band was due to appear on stage. The club's manager came by and asked the men to unlock the door. When they refused, the manager grew suspicious. He called the police, who broke into the room and took everyone, including Mary Ann and the other musicians in the band, to jail, where they spent the night. Charles and three of the musicians had marks on their arms revealing that they had been injecting heroin. Detectives said they had found a syringe and needle along with some marijuana.

In the courtroom, Charles lied about using heroin. He said he was blind and had no idea what was being injected into his arm. He paid several thousand dollars to get the charges against him and the others dropped, although the remaining band members, including Mary Ann, stayed in jail for a week.

Mary Ann loved Charles and it was only for that reason that she put up with his drug use. She hated drugs and refused to try any or learn how to inject Charles, even though he asked her to do both. Charles also occasionally hit her—so hard that on at least one occasion she wound up in the hospital.

Charles continued touring, and he recorded four new songs: "Hallelujah I Love Her So," "What Would I Do Without You," "Drown in My Own Tears," and "Mary Ann." When recording "Drown in My Own Tears," Charles used several teenage girls as backup singers. They were called the Cookies. Charles liked the gospel-like effect they created.

Before working again with the Cookies, Charles made a jazz recording in New York. He worked only with a bass player and drummer and recorded four songs: "Dawn Ray," "Music Music Music," "Black Coffee," and "The Man I Love."

Charles then headed to Atlanta to record more rhythm and blues. He worked the Cookies into every number and was so pleased with the sound that he considered taking them on tour with his band. But Charles was cautious. Unsure of whether he could afford this expense yet, he decided to wait.

Charles was always very careful with his money. He had several bank accounts scattered throughout New York as well as the one he still kept in Greenville, Florida, plus another in Dallas, where his wife lived. Charles stopped in at these banks from time to time just to check and see that his money was still there. He made sure his band expenses did not run too high, and he paid his musicians as little as he could get away with, about thirty dollars a night.

"Whatever little name I had, I'd earned by playing in front of black people."

In the mid-1950s, Charles often encountered prejudice while his band toured, especially in the South. The musicians frequently were unable to use roadside bathrooms or stop at highway restaurants for food because they were African American. When Charles was going to perform in Augusta, Georgia, he learned the audience was to be segregated. White people were given the better downstairs seats while black men and women had to sit upstairs.

"Whatever little name I had," he said, "I'd earned by playing in front of black people. They were the ones who'd been supporting me, and I wasn't about to insult them."[6] Charles asked the tour promoter to allow blacks in the downstairs seats. The promoter would not do this and Charles was fined close to two thousand dollars for breaking his contract by refusing to perform.

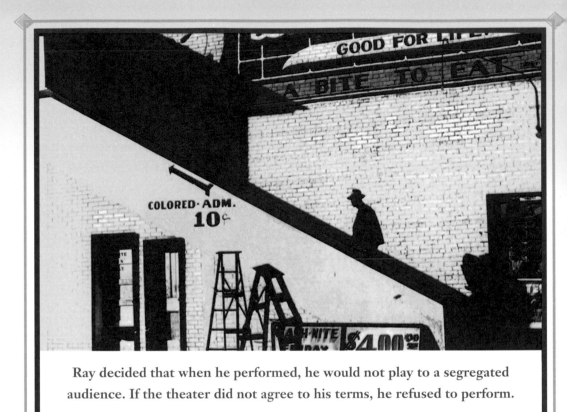

Ray decided that when he performed, he would not play to a segregated audience. If the theater did not agree to his terms, he refused to perform.

◆ ◆ ◆ ◆ ◆

Throughout the late 1950s, Charles recorded new songs about every six months. As he approached his twenty-seventh birthday, his first album, entitled *Ray Charles*, was released. It was made up of songs Charles had recorded as singles, including "Ain't That Love" and "I Got a Woman." Although Charles was becoming recognized by white and black audiences, the album did not sell very well.

Another album, this time a jazz recording, was released by Atlantic in the fall. *The Great Ray Charles* sold well from the start, with white buyers purchasing the recording as well as blacks. The single "Swanee River Rock," based on the old song by Stephen Foster, made it onto *Billboard*'s Top 100 chart in the seventieth spot. It eventually climbed up to the number forty-two spot. This was the first time Charles had a song that was not rhythm and blues appear on a chart.

With his album and singles selling well, Charles watched one of his dreams come true when he performed at a jazz concert at Carnegie Hall in New York City, joining jazz greats Dizzy Gillespie, pianist Thelonious Monk, singer Billie Holiday, and sax player John Coltrane. Although Holiday was at the end of her career, Charles was honored to perform with her.

Meanwhile, Charles had decided it was time to take his female vocalists on the road with the band. He liked what their backup singing added to the group's sound and he changed their name to the Raelets. Charles now traveled with thirteen musicians. His expenses had increased, but his larger band also commanded higher prices at their nightclub performances.

Charles began relationships with some of the women in the band, even though he learned that Della was pregnant with his second child, who would be named David Charles Robinson. Because he was traveling so

Ray at the piano, with his band and his backup vocal group, the Raelets.

much, Charles decided to buy a house in Los Angeles for Della and the children. They moved there in March 1958.

That summer, Charles got a chance to play at the Newport Jazz Festival. Bandleader Duke Ellington, John Coltrane, and trumpeter Miles Davis performed there, along with singers Chuck Berry and Joe Turner. The reviews gave mild praise to Charles's performance, but the audience responded with enthusiasm to his performance of such songs as "Yes Indeed," "I'm a Fool for You," and "I Got a Woman."

The touring continued along with Charles's dependence on heroin and his ongoing relationships with different women. While his habits did not change, his music always was growing and developing. During a performance near Pittsburgh, Pennsylvania, one December evening, Charles discovered that he had nothing left to play that seemed right for the excited crowd. He had already played all the songs that suited the atmosphere and so he simply decided to improvise. "I said to the guys, 'Look, I don't know where I'm going, so y'all follow me,'" Charles said.[7]

He instructed the Raelets to repeat whatever he sang. This was actually a gospel device—having the choir respond to his calls and cries—like a musical question-and-answer. He mixed this with a strong rhythm and blues feel. "I began noodling," he said. "Just a little riff which floated up into my head. It felt good and I kept going."[8]

NEWPORT JAZZ FESTIVAL / NEW YORK
1954-1978 / 25 SUMMERS OF JAZZ
JUNE 23-JULY 2

Ray Charles played at the 1958 Newport Jazz Festival, along with many other jazz and blues greats.

The resulting song was an instant hit with the crowd, many of whom asked where they could find the recording. Charles told them there was no recording; he had made up the song to kill time.

"I try to put all of me into what I am singing or playing," he said. "If I don't feel it, I'd rather just forget the whole business. If I don't believe it myself, I can't make anyone else believe it."[9]

As Charles continued to work on the song through the weeks, perfecting and polishing it, he eventually titled the number "What'd I Say." The song would become the biggest hit of Charles's career.

Chapter 8

The Big Time

T he producers at Atlantic knew they had a hit on their hands when they were working on "What'd I Say." Since the song had grown out of Charles's improvisations, it was not tightly put together at first. Plus, it was very long.

The producers listened to Charles's recording over and over and then went to work. They took out some of Charles's piano solos and also removed several of the Raelets' choruses. When the result still came out too long at six minutes, they decided to divide the song into two parts. One side of the 45-rpm record would be "What'd I Say, Part I," while the other would be "What'd I Say, Part II." Since more records were purchased during the summer than any other time—especially by teenagers—Atlantic decided to release the song in June 1959.

When "What'd I Say" was released, some radio station's executives were reluctant to play it. Charles's moans and shouts, which were echoed by the female chorus moaning and shouting back, struck them as too sexy. Even some of the lyrics seemed too sexy. They did not want to air the song. Atlantic officials changed some of the lyrics and removed others and released it again in July. The song came onto the pop charts at number 82 and within a few weeks climbed to the twenty-sixth spot. By August, it was fifteenth on the pop charts and number one on the rhythm and blues charts. It finally reached the number-six spot for pop and settled into the number-two rhythm and blues spot behind the wildly popular "Mack the Knife."

The song brought Charles the most money in royalties—money paid to a songwriter based on how well a record sells—he had ever earned. It sold so well that, for the first time, Atlantic brought in $1 million in sales in just one month. "What'd I Say" has been considered by many to be Charles's first masterpiece.

By this time, Charles had been touring back and forth across the country for five years. "The road was my life," he said.[1]

He had been voted best "Male Singer-New Star" by the readers of *Down Beat* magazine. His managers at Shaw Artists were now fully aware of just how big Charles could become. Yet he still owed most of his popularity to African-American listeners. To truly make Charles a star, the executives at Shaw knew that he also needed to be popular with white audiences. Although Atlantic was a

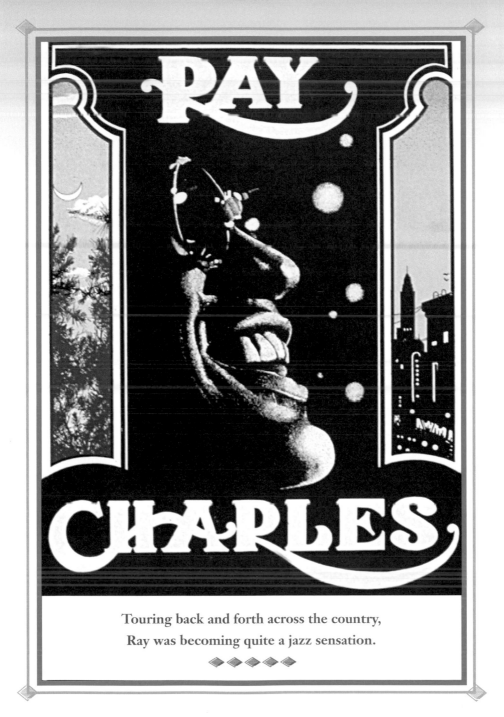

Touring back and forth across the country,
Ray was becoming quite a jazz sensation.

very successful label, it was basically considered a black label.

The people at Shaw decided it was time for Charles to move on, and they were looking at ABC-Paramount Records. Although the company was only a few years old, it was a major name. Signing with ABC-Paramount could launch Charles to the top.

The company was interested in signing Charles, as were many other companies. To encourage Charles to sign with ABC-Paramount, he was offered a special deal that no performing musician had been offered before. Charles was given a contract as the producer of his records. This essentially meant that he now played two roles: performer and businessman. It gave him more money and it also gave him more power. To sweeten the deal, ABC-Paramount also guaranteed Charles fifty thousand dollars a year for the next three years.

> They knew serious drug use could interfere with his production.

To protect themselves, officials at ABC-Paramount put in a clause related to Charles's heroin addiction. They knew serious drug use could interfere with his production, although Charles swore that he would not let this happen. However, ABC-Paramount extended his contract year so that if he did not turn out twelve songs per year, the year would continue until he did.

Charles had been content at Atlantic, but this was a deal he could not refuse. In the fall of 1959, Charles signed with ABC-Paramount. In doing this, he proved something everyone close to him already knew: not only was he a great musician, he was a great businessman.

At this time, Margie Hendricks, one of the Raelets, gave birth to a son. As the father, Charles promised he would support his son, named Charles Wayne.

Charles's business sense extended to the way he managed the band. He had not even turned thirty, yet he held the group together tightly, inspiring everyone with his confidence and motivation to succeed. "He had us spellbound," said saxophonist Bennie "Hank" Crawford. "He was a *general*! And blind! He was young, but we followed him as an older person. He was striking a big chord with the world, and we felt it with him."[2]

At the start of 1960, Charles played to a sellout crowd at the Hollywood Palladium. Advertisements for the performance called him "The Most Creative Musical Giant of the Generation!" Onstage, Charles's performances were as energetic as they were musical. He would sit at the piano, rocking back and forth, and singing in his husky voice with his mouth pressed close to the microphone. As he played, he would nervously shove his sunglasses back on his nose. Although in day-to-day conversation he spoke with a stammer, there was no trace of it when

Charles was singing. And Charles never felt that his blindness got in the way of his career.

"Seeing people or not seeing them, life is still life," he said. "The match that burns you also burns me. I don't need to see to play or sing the way I feel. That comes from within."[3]

Charles was now focusing on which songs to record for his first album for ABC-Paramount. He decided that each song would relate to a specific location. For example, he planned to record "Alabamy Bound" and "California, Here I Come." Almost as an afterthought, he decided to add "Georgia on My Mind," a song by Hoagy Carmichael that Charles had always enjoyed singing.

At the recording session for the album, Charles not only turned up late, he was high on heroin. He had a habit of scratching himself when he was high. As he sat at the piano, he had his latest girlfriend, Mae Mosely, who sang in the Raelets, scratch his feet and ankles until they were bloody. He recorded "Georgia on My Mind" twenty times until he was satisfied with the results. ABC-Paramount called the album *Genius Hits the Road*, planning to release it later in the year.

The touring continued while Charles recorded a second album, *Dedicated to You*. With the first album revolving around place names, this second album focused on women and included such songs as "Sweet Georgia Brown."

● ●

The Business of Music

Charles enjoyed his success, but he was enough of a businessman to know the record—as well as his own popularity—might not last forever. When he had a success on his hands, Charles always based it on one fact, "I work hard," he said.[4] The hard work paid off. By the end of 1960, Charles received a check from ABC-Paramount for $800,000.

In March 1960, *Genius Hits the Road* appeared in stores. After a few months of strong sales, the song "Georgia on My Mind" made it onto *Billboard*'s Hot 100 chart. As the weeks went by, it kept climbing and by early November, the song had taken over the number-four spot. Two weeks later, it reached number one, making it the nation's most popular record.

Yet Charles's drug use, which he had always tried to keep separate from his musical career, was starting to interfere with his work. There were times in early 1960 when he simply did not show up for performances. The reason? He was too high. Excuses were made to audiences about his failure to show up, but anyone who knew Charles knew that heroin was the real reason.

One evening in March, Charles was home in Los Angeles with his wife, Della. He had been shooting up heroin upstairs. Although Della usually did not comment on his drug habit—much as she hated it—she knew what was going on. When little Ray Jr., who was six, asked Della if he could say good night to his father, Della said no. She knew what kind of shape Charles must be in and she did not want the little boy to see him like that.

Ray Jr., however, ignored his mother's advice. He went upstairs and knocked on the door. When his father did not answer, the boy opened the door. Charles was moving frantically around the room, covered with blood. Ray Jr. screamed and Della hurried upstairs. She tried the door, but Charles had locked it. She called two musician friends, who came over immediately. Charles was a large man and he was often difficult to handle when he was on drugs. He scratched and thrashed about.

Della and the musicians found Charles on the floor with his left hand severely cut. Blood was pouring from it and they quickly wrapped it in towels and got him to a doctor. Charles had cut his hand on a glass table and had lost so much blood that he needed a transfusion of four pints of blood. Not only had he cut an artery in his hand, but he had cut a tendon, a band of tissue that connects muscle to bone. The doctor told him it would take six weeks for his hand to heal.

Yet no matter what obstacles presented themselves to Charles throughout his life—even when they were of his own making—he refused to give in to them. Retha had raised him to push through obstacles. "You don't gain anything by giving up," Charles said.[5]

Charles was booked to go on a tour in a week and he was determined to do it. If he could not play piano with two hands, he said, then he would play with one. This is what Charles did and although his hand became infected at one point, it eventually healed.

> If he could not play piano with two hands, he said, then he would play with one.

The tour took Charles through much of the Midwest, finishing in the East at New York's Carnegie Hall. At this time, Charles won his first Grammy Award, for "Georgia on My Mind," and also received an award from the National Association of Recording Arts and Sciences honoring the song as the best pop single in 1960.

While Della gave birth to the couple's third child, a boy named Robert, Charles made his third album for ABC-Paramount. "Ray Charles and Betty Carter" featured Charles and his orchestra along with the singing of Betty Carter. Yet it was a song he recorded after this album that once again put Charles at the top of the charts. "Hit the Road Jack," a foot-tapping rhythm and blues number written by Percy Mayfield, would be released in the fall of 1961.

Until then, Charles again missed a performance in Chicago when police came into an apartment where he was buying heroin. He hid the drugs and spent only a few hours in jail. But once again, heroin had interfered with his work.

His heroin use continued on his first trip to Europe. In Paris, France, Charles was an instant success. He performed at the International Jazz Festival and spent much of his own free time listening to the music of Count Basie and his band. A French music critic wrote that Charles "is forevermore an immortal personality in the history of jazz."[6]

> "I've got to keep moving, keep trying to find something new."

Back in the United States, Charles, as always, was on the go. "I've got to keep moving, keep trying to find something new," he said. "You can't relax. At least, I can't."[7]

When he arrived in Memphis, Tennessee, he learned that the audience was to have separate seating for blacks and whites. Although Charles rarely got involved in civil rights issues, he put his foot down this time. He said he would not perform unless the audience was integrated, with blacks and whites sitting together. He also insisted that signs designating separate bathrooms for blacks be removed. Charles got his way. It was the first time blacks and whites sat together in a public auditorium in Memphis.

At the time that "Hit the Road Jack" was to be released, Mae Mosley gave birth to Charles's daughter.

Tiny Raenee was born with congenital glaucoma, the same disease Charles suffered from.

Executives at ABC-Paramount had expected "Hit the Road Jack" to be a smash hit, and they were right. It leaped onto the pop chart in the fifty-fifth spot and then began to climb. After a few weeks, it made its way to number one and stayed in the top ten for nine weeks. Music critics were calling Charles a major influence in the world of jazz and pop music.[8]

In October 1961, thirty-one-year-old Ray Charles returned to Paris. While the tour was again another enormous success, Charles's drug use was about to catch up with him.

Charles was arrested on drug charges in November 1961.

Chapter 9

The Lows

I n November 1961, Charles was in Indiana for a concert. He was awakened one morning by a knock at the door. When he opened it, the police were there. A drug dealer had told the police they would find evidence of drug use at Charles's place. They did. There were needles used to inject heroin into Charles's arm, capsules that used to contain the drug, and a jar containing marijuana. The police also saw the marks on Charles's arm, indicating his heroin injections.

Charles was taken to the city jail, where he sat on a bench and cried. He said he knew he needed help and should go to a rehabilitation clinic to kick the habit. Publicly, he blamed part of the problem on his blindness. "A guy who lives in the dark has to have something to keep going," he said.[1]

Charles's lawyer bailed him out of jail—that is, he paid money to the authorities as a guarantee that Charles would not run off. So Charles was allowed to continue performing. The story appeared in all the newspapers. At a concert that evening, Charles seemed nervous and jumpy. Reporters asked him numerous questions related to his drug use: How long had he been addicted? How much money did he spend on drugs? Charles answered some questions and avoided others. The truth was that Charles continued using drugs while he toured. Although he made sure to be more careful, he also believed he was wealthy enough to buy his way out of any legal problems. The drug bust in Indiana cost Charles several thousand dollars. But by early 1962, he was just about able to forget it had ever happened. The charges were ultimately dropped when the judge ruled that the police had no proper search warrant and the search had been illegal.

> The drug bust in Indiana cost Charles several thousand dollars.

Charles now focused on two projects he wanted to pursue. One was to make a recording of country music "Ray Charles style." The other was to start his own recording label, Tangerine Records. It was called this because tangerines were Charles's favorite fruit. Not everyone close to Charles was sure an album of country music would sell. After all, his reputation was based on jazz and blues. But Charles had loved country music since he had performed with the Playboys years earlier. His instincts proved correct. "Modern Sounds in Country and Western Music" would become the most popular of his albums to date, with such songs as "Hey Good Lookin'," "Bye Bye Love," and "I Can't Stop Loving You."

"I Can't Stop Loving You" took over the charts in the summer of 1962, sitting at the number-one spot for five weeks. It remained on the charts for a total of eighteen weeks, while the album itself was on the charts for two years and in first place for albums for fourteen weeks. Charles's "experiment" was a smash hit.

More Legal Troubles

Charles had become involved with a receptionist named Sandra Jean Betts in 1962. Betts was pregnant with Charles's child. When she asked him about providing money to pay for the child's upbringing, Charles would not give a definite answer. So Betts went to court to force Charles to pay child support. Charles did not like being forced into anything. He told his lawyer to delay the court proceedings for as long as possible and even denied that he was the father of the child. However, in January 1964 a judge ruled that Charles was the father of Sheila Jean Robinson (born September 1963) and would have to pay four hundred dollars a month to support the child. Charles was not happy about the decision, yet had no choice but to accept it.

Charles launched Tangerine Records in February 1962. He did not plan to use the label for his own records. Instead, he was looking to record established musicians as well as newcomers.

His second country recording, "Modern Sounds Vol. Two," stayed on the charts for sixty-seven weeks, reaching as high as the number-two spot. The hit single from that album was "You Are My Sunshine."

The year 1962 saw Charles as the top recording artist, according to *Billboard* magazine. His single "I Can't Stop Loving You" was the nation's number-one hit of the year and his first volume of country songs was the best-selling album. Charles's earnings from ABC-Paramount for the year totaled $1.6 million. He was at the peak of his popularity.

Charles had been asked to appear in the movie *Ballad in Blue* (also known as *Blues for Lovers*) and he flew to Ireland for the filming. Charles played himself in the movie and he enjoyed the experience. The filming ended in June 1964 and Charles, always on the go, went on a tour throughout the world.

Charles found himself with the band in Boston in late October 1964. At age thirty-four, he now owned his own airplane and after landing at Logan Airport, Charles went to his hotel. Once he was in his room, Charles remembered that his drugs were still on the airplane. Even

From the cellar clubs in London...
to the opening nights
in Paris...
to the wild way out world
of the continental
swingers...
comes a story as different
and exciting as the music
of the man called

RAY
CHARLES
IN
BLUES
FOR
LOVERS

CO-STARRING
TOM BELL
MARY PEACH
DAWN ADDAMS

FEATURING
BETTY McDOWALL LUCY APPLEBY INTRODUCING PIERS BISHOP
PRODUCED BY
HERMAN BLASER
DIRECTED BY PAUL HENREID
ORIGINAL STORY
AND SCREENPLAY BY PAUL HENREID AND BURTON WOHL

AN ALEXANDER SALKIND PRODUCTION   Released by 20th Century-Fox

Charles appeared as himself in this movie.

though it was very early in the morning, Charles asked his driver to take him to the airport.

There were police at the airport and they thought it seemed suspicious that Charles quickly entered and exited his plane at that hour of the morning. Two policemen approached him, asking if they could look in his coat pockets. They found heroin, marijuana, a needle, and a spoon. Charles was arrested and was ordered to appear at a hearing at the end of the week. He was then released.

Charles's luck had finally run out, and he knew it. The story appeared not only in Boston newspapers but all across the United States. Charles could be looking at sixty years in prison and he was scared. If he went to prison, what would that mean for his career? Even apart from his career, Charles worried about being locked up and unable to play music. He was not sure he could exist without music. He realized he had to choose: drugs or music. Eventually he knew the answer. Music meant more to him than anything else.

Although Charles pled not guilty to the charges in U.S. Federal District Court, he was aware that he could be found guilty of the charges he faced. He was being charged with possession of heroin and marijuana and with illegally bringing the drugs into the country.

Charles would not give the names of any of his drug dealers, even though revealing their identities might have helped lighten his possible sentence. If he got off heroin, that might also lessen the sentence.

Charles decided to kick the habit, but he kept shooting up practically until the day he checked himself into a clinic. At that point, he put himself under the care of a physician. He would quit heroin cold turkey—that is, he refused any drugs to ease his withdrawal. "I saw that if I gave up heroin it was going to have to be a deal I made with myself," he said. "No one else could be involved. No promises, no outs, no fancy footwork."[2]

On July 26, 1965, Charles was admitted to St. Francis Hospital in Los Angeles. He was looking for privacy and hoped newspaper reporters would not discover where he was. He had already decided to take the year off from his career, and stories were running in newspapers about the possibility that Charles was ill.

At the hospital, Charles spent four horrible days as his body tried to function without heroin. Heroin withdrawal produces violent symptoms. Charles vomited, had diarrhea, and suffered from severe nausea. Finally, the day came when he could eat some crackers without throwing up. He also slept a lot.

"If I say I'm stopping, I'm stopping!" Charles said. "And that's it! I know I'm gonna be sick for five or six days—which I was—but that'll

"I saw that if I gave up heroin it was going to have to be a deal I made with myself."

Playing chess helped Charles kick his drug
habit. The game became a life-long hobby.

pass. It's all in the attitude, babe. They thought somebody must have been slipping me drugs because I wasn't doing any of the things you're supposed to do. . . . But it was tough, babe, I can tell you that."[3]

He began playing chess with one of the other patients and fell in love with the game. For the rest of his life, Charles would be an enthusiastic—and highly skilled—chess player. He would often set up the chess board between performances at nightclubs.

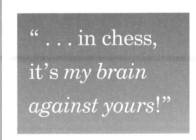

" . . . in chess, it's *my brain against yours!*"

"With cards, no matter how well you play, you ain't gonna win unless the cards fall for you," he explained. "But in chess, it's *my brain against yours*! . . . You've got to outwit, out-think, and out-maneuver the other person, and he's thinking how to outwit you."[4]

Charles finally left the hospital free of his drug addiction. But he still had to deal with his court hearing. This time, on November 22, he pled guilty to the charges against him. The prosecuting attorney asked the judge to sentence Charles to two years in prison and a ten-thousand-dollar fine.

Yet the judge also listened to Charles's lawyer, Paul J. Redmond, who said that "Mr. Charles has successfully for the past five or six months kicked the narcotics habit, that he has great confidence in the people he has been working with, and that they have set out a program that would greatly aid him staying off narcotics."[5]

Redmond added that putting Charles in jail would destroy his career. The judge decided to hold off sentencing Charles for a year. He told Charles that he wanted him to be tested at regular intervals over the next twelve months. Based on the results of these exams, the judge would then decide how to sentence Charles.

Charles was happy. He was safe—for now.

Chapter 10

No Regrets

R ay Charles was back performing by the end of 1965. He was happy to be doing once again what he loved most. Even though he later claimed he did not feel any different being off heroin, those around him said they could see the change. He was not as distant or removed. He seemed more *real*.

"I didn't do this for anybody but me," he said about kicking his drug habit. "You have to wanna do it so bad that nothing else matters. It's not like sayin', 'I'm gonna stop smoking.' And it won't do any good for me to tell people about it. What I did ain't gonna inspire nobody."[1]

He gathered his musicians and resumed a hectic touring schedule. In the spring of 1966, he had to get tested so the courts could determine whether his body was still free of heroin. The exam took place in Boston and lasted three days, which was long enough for doctors to observe signs of withdrawal from heroin if Charles still had been using the drug. But he had not gone back to his old habits. Friends later realized that Charles substituted alcohol for

Charles was very happy to be back playing music in 1965.

heroin and was drinking round-the-clock. However, he had not gone back to heroin and at the end of the testing, Charles was told he was free until the fall, when he would be sentenced.

Charles's heavy schedule of cross-country touring plus recording consumed his life again. Singles such as "Let's Go Get Stoned" and "I Choose to Sing the Blues" made their way onto the charts and sold well. At the age of thirty-six, Charles had sold more than 15 million records, and composed more than one hundred songs. He was considered not only an incredible singer, but one of the great jazz pianists.

Charles also continued playing chess, which he had enjoyed ever since his stay in the Los Angeles hospital. "You could wake me up out of a sound sleep to play chess, and dig it, I love my sleep," he said.[2]

He played chess every Sunday at his Los Angeles home, inviting friends over for matches that lasted from ten in the morning until midnight. Della provided the food while Charles would feel the pieces with his fingers, lean back in his chair, and consider his next move. Whoever lost the game had to leave the table and another player would take his place. Charles even set a time limit for a person to move, to keep the games moving faster. These days were filled with talk and laughter. Although Charles lost occasionally, he did not lose often.

Ray and Della with their three young sons

Charles enjoyed experimenting with different genres of music as much as ever. "The challenge is to stay abreast of what's going on around you," he later said. "That doesn't mean you have to be what's happening around you. I mean, I'm not a rapper, and I will never get into that because it isn't me. But I know what's going on with it. What I do is stay current within my type of music. . . . I keep it fresh."[3]

While Charles would always be tied to blues, jazz, and gospel, he also had fun doing his own arrangements of songs by the Beatles. His recording of "Yesterday" hit the number twenty-five spot on the charts. Beatles members John Lennon and Paul McCartney liked Charles's arrangement so much that they sent him a telegram telling Charles they loved him.

In 1968, Charles appeared in a CBS production called *Of Black America*, a television show about the achievements of African Americans. Charles talked about the kind of music he played and its origins. Millions of viewers also watched Charles on television when he appeared in Coca-Cola commercials. These commercials were taped with Aretha Franklin, a celebrated gospel, soul, and rhythm-and-blues singer.

Although Charles himself was a musical celebrity throughout the country and much of the world, his records were not selling quite as well as they had in the past. By the end of the 1960s, Charles had not had a best-selling single or album in several years. Sales were poor for his two newest albums, *I'm All Yours, Baby*, a romantic collection of songs and *Ray Charles Doing His Thing*, a lively rhythm-and-blues album.

Regardless of sales, Charles continued recording. His own label, Tangerine Records, came out with *Volcanic Action of My Soul*. The 1971 album was filled with beautiful songs that did not center around a theme as had most of Charles's previous records. It made it as far as number fifty-two on the charts. That same year, ABC Records released *A 25th Anniversary in Show Business Salute to Ray Charles*. The album's name made it sound as if Charles was old and had been around forever. His 1972 album *A Message from the People* also hit number fifty-two and included his well-known version of the song "America the Beautiful." Charles's last recording on the Tangerine label was "Through the Eyes of Love," which was released at the end of the year.

By the middle of the 1970s, Charles's marriage to Della came to an end. The couple had been married for twenty-one years. Throughout that time, Charles's relationships with other women had been difficult for Della to tolerate. Charles paid child support and gave Della thirty-five hundred dollars a month to live on, plus she kept their large home in Los Angeles.

Charles's life continued as it had before. He appeared on several television variety shows and even put in appearances on *Sesame Street* and the game show *Hollywood Squares*. As Charles approached his fiftieth birthday, he wrote his autobiography, *Brother Ray*. The book received good reviews and sold well. He had worked on the book with Texas journalist David Ritz. The men got together a couple of times a week and Ritz even went on the road with the band. Charles demanded approval of everything that would appear in the book.

Charles had fun with the Muppets on *Sesame Street*.

When Ritz first began meeting with Charles to put together his autobiography, he would say, "Now if this question is too tough . . ." But Charles consistently answered, "How can a question be too tough? The truth is the truth."[4]

While Charles's successes were small in the 1970s compared to previous decades, he kept exploring new possibilities and looking for new challenges. He had no interest in slowing down. "I've known times where I've felt terrible," he said, "but once I get to the stage and the band starts with the music, I don't know why but it's like you have pain and take an aspirin, and you don't feel it no more."[5]

He made an appearance in the hit movie *The Blues Brothers*, starring John Belushi and Dan Aykroyd and, as always, was working on a new album. The 1980s did not produce many hits and Charles looked to move in other directions. His performances began to include a full orchestra. In 1980, for example, he went onstage with the Boston Pops under conductor John Williams.

Many people were surprised to see Charles—who claimed to be a Democrat—play at the Republican National Convention in Dallas in 1984. After his performance of "America the Beautiful," Charles stood with President Ronald Reagan and Vice President George H. W. Bush, smiling for the television cameras. In 1985, he made a recording of "We Are the World" with

Charles appeared in *The Blues Brothers* with John
Belushi, right, and Dan Aykroyd, left.

Bruce Springsteen, Michael Jackson, Billy Joel, and Bob
Dylan to benefit famine relief.

"I don't have no mountains left to climb or oceans to
cross," Charles said. "See, although I've had a lot of trou-
bles in my life, I have to be very honest and tell you I've
been a blessed man.[6]

"I don't think of myself as a strong rock 'n' roller,"
Charles said;

> But I don't want to minimize the honor. . . . I think
> of myself as a good utility person, like baseball.

In 1985, Charles (center with sunglasses) was one of forty-five
top recording artists who joined together to produce a record to
raise money for starving people in Africa.

◆ ◆ ◆ ◆ ◆

I'm not a specialist. I'm not a blues singer, jazz singer
or country singer. I am a singer who sings blues,
country and jazz. Also, I can handle a lot of different
things: writing, composing, arranging. I'm an all-
around type.[7]

In 1987, he was given the Lifetime Achievement honor
at the Grammy Awards. At fifty-eight years of age, Charles
was still working as hard as ever and keeping his usual
rigorous schedule of performing and recording.

"Take it easy? Music is like a part of me," he said,

> It's not something I do on the side. It's like my bloodline, like my breathing apparatus. I think the people that worry about things like aging are pretty silly. If the day comes when I don't got it no more, that's it. . . . My voice right now is in the best shape it has ever been [in]. I can make it do anything I want right now. How long will that last? I'll just enjoy it while I can.[8]

The Honors Pour In

In 1986, Charles was honored by the Kennedy Center for the Performing Arts. He was also inducted that year into the Rock and Roll Hall of Fame. The museum of that organization is located in Cleveland, Ohio, and inducts a small number of rock and roll musicians every year. Charles was among the first ten musicians inducted, a list that included Chuck Berry, Elvis Presley, and Buddy Holly.

Not only did Charles still enjoy it, he was as much of a perfectionist as ever. "Do it right or don't do it at all. That comes from my mom," Charles said,

> If there's something I want to do, I'm one of those people that won't be satisfied until I get it done. If I'm trying to sing something and I can't get it, I'm gonna keep at it till I get it where I want it because I hate to leave things half-done. If I was gonna clean this room right now, I'd clean the whole room. I wouldn't clean half of it. I'm just that way.[9]

During a performance in California with his band, fifty-eight-year-old Charles noticed that one of his horn players was not keeping proper time. He said something to the musician in the middle of the performance, calling out from his piano bench. "When something happens, they hear about it right then. If I try to wait till later on, I might forget," Charles said. "I don't build a case out of it. We have some new people in the band right now. They're learning, and they understand it's not the kind of thing where somebody's bent out of shape."[10]

Although Charles had continued to turn out albums, his greatest success in later life came when he did commercials for Diet Pepsi in the early 1990s. The line "You've got the right one, baby, uh-huh" swept the nation and the ad stayed on television for two years.

When President Clinton was inaugurated in January 1993, Charles sang "America the Beautiful" at the inaugural gala. Clinton had recently presented Charles with the National Medal of Arts at the White House. Other recipients included playwright Arthur Miller and movie director Billy Wilder.

In 2003, Charles had surgery to replace his hip. His health began to fail as he was recovering from this operation, and it was during that time that he was diagnosed with liver failure.

"I've been a blessed man," said Ray Charles.

"I ain't going to live forever," he said. "I got enough sense to know that. I also know it's not a question of how long I live, but it's a question of how well I live."[11]

In the weeks before he died, Charles still kept up his usual routine. Although he was in great pain, he went to his studio every day. A bed had been set up for him at the studio and he was surrounded by nurses. But Charles was determined to try to live what was left of his life exactly as he had done in the past.

Charles attended a ceremony on April 30, 2004, when his recording studios on Washington Boulevard in Los Angeles were named an historic landmark by the city. That was his last public appearance.

Ray Charles died on June 10, 2004, at age seventy-three. The cause of death was liver disease. Charles had turned out more than one hundred albums over the course of six decades. He is remembered not only as a musical legend, but as a man who overcame every obstacle he confronted.

"Every experience I've had, good or bad, has taught me something," he said. "I was born a poor boy in the South. I'm black, I'm blind, I once fooled around with drugs, but all of it was like going to school. And I've tried to be a good student. I don't regret a damn thing."[12]

Chronology

1930—Ray Charles Robinson is born in Albany, Georgia.

1936—His brother, George, drowns in a washtub.

1937—Ray loses his eyesight.

1945—His mother, Retha Robinson, dies.

1948—Ray leaves Florida and moves to Seattle, Washington.

1949—Hits the charts with "Confession Blues."

1952—Signs with Atlantic Records.

1953—Stepmother, Mary Jane Robinson, dies.

1955—His song "I Got a Woman" hits number two on the R&B charts.

Marries Della Howard.

Ray Charles Robinson, Jr. born on May 25.

1956—"Drown in My Own Tears" reaches number one on rhythm and blues charts.

1957—Debut album *Ray Charles* is released.

1958—Makes successful appearance at Newport Jazz Festival.

1960—"Georgia on My Mind" becomes number-one pop hit.

1962—Forms Ray Charles Enterprises, which includes Tangerine Records.

1964—Is arrested on drug charges at Logan Airport; enters rehabilitation clinic the next year.

1978—Autobiography, *Brother Ray*, is published.

1979—"Georgia on My Mind" becomes Georgia's state song.

1986—Is inducted into the Rock and Roll Hall of Fame.

1994—Wins his twelfth Grammy Award, for "A Song for You."

2004—Dies of complications of liver disease on June 10 in Beverly Hills, California.

Grammy Awards

1960—Best Vocal Performance Single Record or Track, Male, "Georgia on My Mind"

Best Performance by a Pop Single Artist, "Georgia on My Mind"

Best Rhythm and Blues Performance, "Let the Good Times Roll"

Best Vocal Performance Album, Male, *The Genius of Ray Charles*

1961—Best Rhythm and Blues Recording, "Hit the Road Jack"

1962—Best Rhythm and Blues Recording, "I Can't Stop Loving You"

1963—Best Rhythm and Blues Recording, "Busted"

1966   Best Rhythm and Blues Recording, "Crying Time"

Best Rhythm and Blues Solo Vocal Performance, "Crying Time"

RAY CHARLES

1975—Best Rhythm and Blues Vocal Performance, Male, "Living for the City"

1990—Best Rhythm and Blues Performance by a Duo or Group with Vocal, "I'll Be Good to You" (with Chaka Khan)

1993—Best Rhythm and Blues Vocal Performance, Male, "A Song for You"

Discography

A Selected List

The Genius of Ray Charles (1959; rereleased Madacy
Records, 1999)

What'd I Say (1959; rereleased Wea, 2004)

The Genius Hits the Road (1960; rereleased Rhino
Records, 1997)

Modern Sounds in Country and Western Music (1962;
rereleased Rhino Records, 1988)

Ultimate Hits Collection (Rhino Records, 1999)

The Very Best of Ray Charles (Rhino Records, 2000)

Genius After Hours (Wea/Rhino, 2001)

Genius Loves Company (Concord Jazz, 2004)

I Got a Woman (Universe, 2004)

Birth of a Legend: Complete Early Recordings (Blue Moon,
2005).

Brother Ray (Wonderful Music Of, 2005)

Classic Years (Comet, 2005)

Essential (Newsound, 2005)

Genius and Friends (Atlantic, 2005)

I Chose to Sing the Blues (BCI Music, 2005)

In Concert (Movieplay Gold, 2005)

Live at the Olympia 2000 (Phantom Imports, 2004)

Chapter Notes

Chapter 1. Searching for Success
1. Taylor Hackford and James L. White, *Ray: A Tribute to the Movie, the Music, and the Man* (New York: Newmarket Press, 2004), p. 37.
2. Ray Charles and David Ritz, *Brother Ray: Ray Charles' Own Story* (New York: The Dial Press, 1978), p. 100.

Chapter 2. Early Hardships
1. Ray Charles and David Ritz, *Brother Ray: Ray Charles' Own Story* (New York: The Dial Press, 1978), p. 8.
2. Michael Lydon, *Ray Charles: Man and Music* (New York: Riverhead Books, 1998), p. 8.
3. Thomas Thompson, "Music Soaring in a Darkened World," *Life*, July 29, 1966, p. 61.
4. Charles and Ritz, p. 47.
5. Ibid., p. 11.
6. Thompson, p. 62.

Chapter 3. Boarding School
1. Ray Charles and David Ritz, *Brother Ray: Ray Charles' Own Story* (New York: The Dial Press, 1978), p. 20.
2. Michael Lydon, *Ray Charles: Man and Music* (New York: Riverhead Books, 1998), p. 14.
3. Charles and Ritz, p. 31.
4. Ibid., p. 34.
5. Ibid., p. 35.

6. Lawrence Christon, "Ray Charles: Proud to Be a Legend," *Los Angeles Times*, December 24, 1986, p. 1.

7. Lydon, p. 20.

8. Charles and Ritz, pp. 41–42.

9. Lydon, p. 23.

10. Christon, p. 1.

Chapter 4: On His Own

1. Ray Charles and David Ritz, *Brother Ray: Ray Charles' Own Story* (New York: The Dial Press, 1978), p. 67.

2. Lawrence Christon, "Ray Charles: Proud to Be a Legend," *Los Angeles Times*, December 24, 1986, p. 1.

3. Ibid.

4. Scott Benarde, "Ray Charles Earning All-Around Acclaim," *Sun Sentinel*, Fort Lauderdale, December 26, 1986, p. 45.

5. Charles and Ritz, pp. 180–181.

6. Michael Lydon, *Ray Charles: Man and Music* (New York: Riverhead Books, 1998), p. 43.

7. Charles and Ritz, p. 94.

Chapter 5. On the Move

1. Ray Charles and David Ritz, *Brother Ray: Ray Charles' Own Story* (New York: The Dial Press, 1978), p. 108.

2. Adam Bernstein, "A Singular Blend of Styles; Keyboardist, Composer, Singer Won 12 Grammys," *The Washington Post*, June 11, 2004, p. A12.

3. Charles and Ritz, p. 120.

4. Phil Kloer, "Death of a Soul Icon: Ray Charles: Sept. 23, 1930–June 10, 2004: Crying Time Georgia Native's Stirring Music Spanned Genres, Decades," *The Atlanta Journal–Constitution*, June 11, 2004, p. C1.

CHAPTER NOTES

Chapter 6. A Sound of His Own

1. Richard Crawford, *America's Musical Life: A History* (New York: Norton, 2001), p. 725.

2. Jon Pareles, "Ray Charles, Who Reshaped American Music, Dies at 73," *New York Times*, June 10, 2004, p. A1.

3. Michael Lydon, *Ray Charles: Man and Music* (New York: Riverhead Books, 1998), p. 105.

4. Ibid., p. 109.

Chapter 7. Higher and Higher

1. Mark Feeney, "Ray Charles, Legend of Soul, Dies. American Master of Styles was 73," *Boston Globe*, June 11, 2004, p. C14.

2. Taylor Hackford and James L. White, *Ray: A Tribute to the Movie, the Music, and the Man* (New York: Newmarket Press, 2004), p. 102.

3. Richard Cromelin and Randy Lewis, "Ray Charles: 1930–2004; 'The Genius' Put His Stamp on Music, From Soul to Country," *Los Angeles Times*, June 11, 2004, p. A1.

4. Michael Lydon, *Ray Charles: Man and Music* (New York: Riverhead Books, 1998), p. 120.

5. Ray Charles and David Ritz, *Brother Ray: Ray Charles' Own Story* (New York: The Dial Press, 1978), p. 163.

6. Ibid., p. 164.

7. Lydon, p. 153.

8. Charles and Ritz, p. 191.

9. Hackford and White, p. 19.

Chapter 8. The Big Time

1. Ray Charles and David Ritz, *Brother Ray: Ray Charles' Own Story* (New York: The Dial Press, 1978), p. 186.

2. Michael Lydon, *Ray Charles: Man and Music* (New York: Riverhead Books, 1998), p. 172.

3. "One of the 'Immortals,'" *Newsweek*, November 13, 1961, p. 96.

4. Lydon, p. 175.

5. Ibid., p. 341.

6. "One of the 'Immortals,'" p. 96.

7. Ibid.

8. Ibid.

Chapter 9. The Lows

1. Michael Lydon, *Ray Charles: Man and Music* (New York: Riverhead Books, 1998), p. 208.

2. Ray Charles and David Ritz, *Brother Ray: Ray Charles' Own Story* (New York: The Dial Press, 1978), p. 256.

3. Jane Wollman Rusoff, "The Soul of Ray Charles," *Sun Sentinel*, Fort Lauderdale, Florida, July 5, 1998, p. 8.

4. Lydon, p. 255.

5. Thomas Thompson, "Music Soaring in a Darkened World," *Life*, July 29, 1966, p. 58.

Chapter 10. No Regrets

1. Thomas Thompson, "Music Soaring in a Darkened World," *Life*, July 29, 1966, p. 58.

2. Lawrence Christon, "Ray Charles: Proud to Be a Legend," *Los Angeles Times*, December 24, 1986, p. 9.

3. Jane Wollman Rusoff, "The Soul of Ray Charles," *Sun Sentinel*, Fort Lauderdale, Florida, July 5, 1998, p. 8.

CHAPTER NOTES

4. Taylor Hackford and James L. White, *Ray: A Tribute to the Movie, the Music, and the Man* (New York: Newmarket Press, 2004), p. 189.

5. Adam Bernstein, "A Singular Blend of Styles; Keyboardist, Composer, Singer Won 12 Grammys," *The Washington Post*, June 11, 2004, p. A1.

6. Phil Kloer, "Death of a Soul Icon: Ray Charles: Sept. 23, 1930–June 10, 2004: Crying Time Georgia Native's Stirring Music Spanned Genres, Decades," *The Atlanta Journal–Constitution*, June 11, 2004, p. C1.

7. Scott Benarde, "Ray Charles Earning All-Around Acclaim," *Sun Sentinel*, Fort Lauderdale, Florida, December 26, 1986, p. 45.

8. Mike Boehm, "Ray Charles at Crazy Horse Freer, More Physical Than at Arts Center," *Los Angeles Times*, June 2, 1988, p. 11.

9. Jane Wollman Rusoff, "The Soul of Ray Charles," *Sun Sentinel*, Fort Lauderdale, Florida, July 5, 1998, p. 8.

10. Mike Boehm, "Ray Charles at Crazy Horse Freer, More Physical Than at Arts Center," *Los Angeles Times*, June 2, 1988, p. 11.

11. Jon Pareles, "Ray Charles, Who Reshaped American Music, Dies at 73," *New York Times*, June 10, 2004, p. A1.

12. Kloer, p. C1.

Further Reading

Beyer, Mark. *Ray Charles*. New York: Rosen Central, 2003.

Mathis, Sharon Bell. *Ray Charles*. New York: Lee & Low Books, 2001.

Quill, Charles G. *The History of the Blues*. New York: Rosen Publishing Group: 2003.

Internet
Addresses

Legends of American Music: Ray Charles
   <http://www.swingmusic.net/Ray_Charles_
    Biography.html>

Official Ray Charles Web site
   <http://www.raycharles.com/index.html>

Ray Charles on the History of Rock Web site
   <http://www.history-of-rock.com/ray_charles.
    htm>

Index

Page numbers for photographs are in **boldface** type.

INDEX